divine magic

André &
Lynette Singer

divine
magic

the world of the
supernatural

VIEWER
BOOKS
™

ACKNOWLEDGEMENTS

It would take an element of magic to thank all the many people who contributed towards the making of this book. It began with Stuart Rekant and his idea for a film series and expanded into a creative enterprise spanning four continents. We would especially like to thank James Mitchell and Sarah Mahaffy for their unwavering support through the uncertain months of development, Susanna Wadeson for her thoughtfulness and editorial wisdom and Nicky Paris for the gentle humour with which she undertook the huge job of researching the pictures. Our gratitude goes also to Lenny Abrahamson, Rebecca Cody, John Paul Davidson, Katherine Leach-Lewis, Sylvia van Kleef, Robyn O'Brien, Judy Patterson, Howard Reid, Steve Seidenberg, John Sheppard, Peter Spry-Leverton, Richard Thomson, Sarah Thomson, Graham Townsley, Melanie Wangler and Hugo Young for all their help. Thanks to TV Books and The Discovery Channel.
Lastly, our thanks to our families and our friends in Kew, for their kindness, interest, and forbearance.
For Picture Acknowledgements see page 192.

Ψ   Ψ

This is a Viewer Book
Published by TV Books, Inc.
1995

Published in the United States by TV Books Inc., New York.
Distributed to the trade by Penguin USA, New York.

Viewer Books
TV Books, Inc.
1995 Broadway
New York, NY10023

Publisher's Cataloging in Publication
Singer, Andre, 1945-
Divine magic: the world of the supernatural / Andre & Lynette Singer.
  p. cm.
  Includes bibliographical references and index.
  ISBN: 1-57500-001-6
  1. Supernatural. 2. Occultism. I. Singer, Lynette. II. Title.
BF1031.S56 1995   133
                             QB195-20326

Divine Magic™ is a Non Fiction Films presentation of
a Café/Little Bird production, with the support of Eurimages.
The series is produced by André Singer.
James Mitchell and Stuart B Rekant are Executive Producers.

CONTENTS

Ψ

Ψ

INTRODUCTION

There has never been a society without some concept of the supernatural, some awareness of forces moving in the shadows beyond human understanding. Our efficient, science-driven modern society is no exception. Although our society is the first without a formal belief system, we are filled with a fascination for the supernatural, a guaranteed interest in paranormal events, and a burning desire to know what might be really going on. Lacking a coherent system to inform us about the great human questions – our place in the cosmos, in time, our purpose, and our ultimate destination – we surge from fashion to fashion, trying each new solution and moving restlessly on. The questions are still the same: what controls our destiny, and how can we influence the outcome?

We all need to make some sense of the world; to understand, predict, and influence it. Unfortunately we do not find the world quite so tidily arranged, and our best efforts to understand it still leave us with much to explain. Some aspects proved to be amenable to scientific study, and during the 19th and 20th centuries the societies of western Europe and America made great strides in developing theories of causation and in extending their understanding of natural laws. There were huge advances in physics, chemistry, biology, astronomy, and medicine, and mankind learned more about the physical world and devised more ways of employing that knowledge than in all the previous centuries of human existence. It is not surprising that it was so readily assumed that science could and would explain everything, given time.

Human culture is, however, multifaceted; no single analysis could hope to deal with the complexities of its concerns. Twentieth-century wisdom suggests to us that everything in our world can and should be understandable in terms of the laws of science; that we should use only the scientific method in arriving at our conclusions. Yet one of

Ψ

Ψ

ABOVE: Hokusai's 19th-century Japanese ghost, returning to observe his wife and her lover.

the most human of characteristics is the ability to believe, to have certainties that are not supported by tangible evidence. Out of this capacity have grown art, literature, music, religion, and a cluster of beliefs and practises known as the supernatural. These have existed throughout history and across the world in every known culture.

The time of expansion in scientific thinking coincided with other voyages of discovery. Western travellers were systematically reaching and observing other, smaller-scale societies dotted about the globe. Here it became obvious that a dual system of explanation was in operation. People in every culture, whatever their level of scientific sophistication, know that unsupported objects fall to the ground, that matter does not readily alter from one form to another and that some processes, such as death, are irreversible. But these cultures had conceded that, in some circumstances, events do not follow this predictable pattern. They believed that operating in tandem with the system which makes apples fall is another which can temporarily over-ride it. In the grip of their new scientific fervour, Western thinkers found it fashionable to deride this view. Other ways of regarding the world were perceived as primitive, flawed versions of scientific reasoning which should be abandoned in favour of rationalism. Apples *must* fall to the ground, the West was convinced, and anyone who thought they might ever do otherwise was either ignorant or deluded. Much was overlooked in this simplistic analysis, notably the distinction between belief and knowledge and the possibility that societies everywhere have their own reasons for adopting more than one world-view. In the rush to adopt scientific rationalism, the harvest of thousands of years of spiritual development was plowed back into the ground.

But it is some centuries since the natural laws were first established; during this time there has certainly been a decrease in religious belief and practise, at least in Western societies, but not the wholesale abandonment which might have been expected. And where mainstream religions have lost, less established areas of belief have gained. Cults have sprung up all over the Western world, superstitions thrive, magic and the occult enjoy new waves of popularity, and interest and curiosity about any aspect of the supernatural run at fever pitch. Anything from crop circles to bigfoots can take over the mass media, and switchboards jam after radio and television items featuring unexplained events. This does not seem like a culture which has thoroughly embraced science and rationalism.

The inescapable conclusion is that our need to believe is as strong as ever, and that we have a positive requirement to consider our world in nonscientific terms. We seem to need to believe in fantastic events, superhuman powers, and supernatural forces; we are unable to give them up and content ourselves with rationalist explanations. Part of the answer lies in the persistence with which unexplainable events do continue to occur. There is an overwhelming mass of evidence which suggests that not everything in our world fits the convenient categories of science, and that some occurrences fly directly in the face of its laws. Possible ways of dealing with these inexplicable events include denying that they occur or putting them down to fraud or hysteria. But there are far too many instances where this cannot be done, and therefore to deny absolutely the existence of these puzzles is as much a statement of belief as anything declared by those who have experienced them.

Without question, belief, however, is unfashionable in the 20th-century West, and it is easy to see why it can be complicated. Efficient communication has paraded in front of us every variation and shade of belief. All seem equally valid, or equally invalid. Relativism has robbed us of certainty. How much simpler to dwell in a culture where there is no room for doubt; where belief is a straightforward matter of absorbing what we learn in childhood. We find ourselves with the will to believe, but in deep confusion about *what* to believe. To this problem we apply our new assumption that truth can be established scientifically, and so confront all the unexplained areas of our lives with the burden of proof. In this we overlook the fact that belief is not the same as knowledge and that it may serve a very different function in our lives; as the 20th-century Austrian philosopher Ludwig Wittgenstein observed, "We feel that even when all possible scientific questions have been answered, the problems of life remain completely untouched."

This book looks at the main areas where human societies confront the unexplained action of unknown powers; where people try to communicate with these forces, whether envisioned as gods or spirits; try to influence them through magic and ritual; and try to see into the future and deal with death and the afterlife. Taking examples from all over the world and as far back as recorded time allows, we trace the common strands of supernatural experience and ask what, if any, light we have shed upon these recurring questions.

The area to which most accounts of the supernatural address themselves is that of verification. In the best Western tradition they ask, "Is it true?" This, apart from the weeding out of obvious frauds, is possibly the least important question. Even in cases of outright trickery, it is just as interesting to ask *why* people were and are so willing to believe such thinly substantiated cases. But our assumptions about the nature of truth are themselves coming under scrutiny. Science itself is now revealing that the natural world is more complex than we had thought and its laws less straightforward. New theories challenge long-held ideas about cause and effect, and physicists grapple with innovatory conclusions about time and space. International scientific conferences regularly discuss the existence of other dimensions and parallel universes. Most of these debates discuss matter and forces in ways which are, to the layman, more fantastic than anything reported from the observers of the supernatural. What we can never overestimate is the power of the human mind. It can cause a diseased body to heal and a healthy body to die, over-riding all scientific prediction. Hypnosis can cause people to see things which are not there, believe things which have not happened and respond in ways usually foreign to them. If these things can happen, then many others may be possible too.

CHAPTER I

REACHING OUT

ABOVE: A Haitian voodoo ceremony. Possessed by powerful spirits, followers can transcend fear and pain.

Anyone who has been to the cinema in the last 20 years can tell you all about voodoo. It is dark and terrifying, and involves grotesque dolls, dancing skeletons, zombies, and death-inducing curses. This sinister stereotype would not, however, be acceptable to the more than 50 million people in Africa, Haiti, and the United States who are now active in voodoo cults. They see their religion as an uplifting, supportive belief system which focuses on healing, curing, and caring, on both a community and an individual level. Unsurprisingly, present-day followers of voodoo resent the negative connotations which Hollywood has given their religion, while admitting that some aspects of voodoo practise in the past may have provided the seed for these overblown images. The real voodoo is much less lurid than films and novels would have us believe; it is none the less a dramatic religion whose followers communicate with the spirit world, becoming literally as one with the forces which they believe determine their everyday lives.

ABOVE: The image of Baron Samedi, a voodoo spirit associated with death and cemeteries.

TRUE VOODOO

Most people associate voodoo with Haiti, where it is has received much publicity, but today's voodoo followers are spread much more widely. In Africa, the continent in which voodoo had its roots, its influence remains undiminished; the belief flourishes in Nigeria, and since 1990 Benin (formerly Dahomey) has permitted and even encouraged voodoo, after years of repression under a Marxist regime. Across the USA there has been a resurgence of voodoo, with numbers swelled by white, middle-class Americans; a black religion, suppressed by whites, has not only survived but has begun to recruit from its traditional enemies.

RIGHT: Voodoo drummers in Benin, West Africa. Drumming is an essential part of the build-up to ceremonies.

Modern voodoo is a syncretic religion, formed from elements moulded together by time and necessity. Its beginnings lay in West Africa, where the supernatural is viewed as an integral part of daily life. For members of these indigenous societies their ancestors are linked with the living in an unbroken line connecting everyone to the homeland. The spirits of the dead, residing in trees, waterfalls, and ponds, exercise continuing influence over the living. Health, fortune, and success are all affected by relationships with ancestors, but they are at least accessible; it is possible to communicate with the spirits and thus have some power over one's destiny.

Above the plethora of individual ancestors are "super-spirits" or *loas*, which are grouped into pantheons or *vodu*. There is a creator and overall deity, *Gran Met*, but such a god is too remote and inaccessible for humans to reach and it is to the *loas* that mortals must turn. Communication with the *loas* helps with difficulties and protects against the evil intent of others. Each follower identifies with a *vodu* and, with the help of its priests and priestesses, selects a suitable *loa* through which to influence the events of his or her own life. The priests act both as ritual experts and intermediaries between humans and loas. During ceremonies of drumming and dancing they help individuals achieve an ecstatic trance state in which they are taken over by the *loas*. The priests and priestesses remain detached from the trance and possession states sought by their charges, and interpret the actions and wishes of the spirits.

Spirit possession is the ultimate communication between the living and the dead, and through this union the power of the spirits is directed toward the solving of human problems. But care is needed, because the *loas* themselves have a malevolent side, some more than others. The *Guedes*, the gods of darkness, death, and debauchery, also govern the preservation and renewal of life and the growth of children. Their power is needed by humans, but they must be carefully approached if their dangerous side is to be controlled.

This was the belief system which West Africans took with them when they were transported to America and the Caribbean as slaves in the 17th and 18th centuries. They needed a supportive religion in their new life. Those who survived the nightmare voyage on overcrowded slave ships found themselves subjected to every kind of deprivation and hardship. Powerless in almost every area of their lives, they were denied the most basic human rights. Their powerful, almost ecstatic religion was harshly suppressed by slave owners, who saw it as a threat to their control. Where West Africans were mixed with slaves from other societies their religion generally failed to survive, although pockets of voodoo practise survived around New Orleans and as far north as Detroit and Chicago.

ABOVE: A voodoo doll in a Haitian graveyard. Voodoo can be used malevolently, and its powers are widely feared.

In Haiti and the Dominican Republic, however, voodoo fared better; the slaves transported to these countries included a heavy concentration of West African believers and, although they had been wrenched away from their relatives and kin groups, they could still find a group of *vodu* devotees to join. As in America, their religion was forbidden and an edict of 1704 prohibited them from "gathering at night under the pretext of holding collective dances." Catholicism was forced on them as a substitute, and from 1663 plantation owners were obliged by law to baptize their slaves and hold Christian services. But Voodoo was too deep-seated to disappear so easily. The slaves of Haiti reacted by lowering the visibility of their religion and incorporating suitably adjusted European beliefs to satisfy the local government; Catholic elements were simply added onto the pre-existing rituals, and even now voodoo ceremonies include Christian saints and prayers. The Caribs, the indigenous people of Haiti and the Dominican Republic, died out soon after the colonists arrived. But before this happened elements of their religious life, too, had been incorporated into voodoo. By these means the Haitian slaves evolved a religion which satisfied a desperate need, something which their masters could not take away, despite their most determined efforts. The slaves could be taken over by the voodoo spirits and leave their hard and bitter life behind. They could tap into the source of power and use it to envision a different future.

Followers of voodoo believe that each person has two parts to their non-physical self. The first, the *gros bon ange*, is the life force, associated with the breath and the shadow. The second, the *'ti bon ange*, is the spirit or essence of the person, the part that makes the personality. It is sometimes called the *zombie*, and this is the part of the spirit which is most at risk from sorcerers. It lingers for about seven days after death, when it is at its most vulnerable. The popular notion of zombies derives from

RIGHT: Haitian art is rich in voodoo symbolism. Here an early follower comes under the disapproving eye of the law.

Ψ

Ψ

ABOVE: The Haitian Felicia Mentor, widely believed to have been a zombie and photographed here many years after her supposed death and burial.

the belief that sorcerers who had captured a dead person's *'ti bon ange* during the vulnerable week after death could bring the body back to life and use it as slave labor. This idea inspired dread and horror, since it meant that the unfortunate person would never find rest, not even after death. Many Haitians claim to have known zombies, and there are accounts of cases where people do appear to have been resurrected, as well as of those who have sincerely believed themselves to be zombies. Voodoo sorcerers are well versed in herbalism and familiar with poisons. They can administer drugs which simulate death and enable the victim to be buried, then resurrected. Constantly drugged and intimidated, the victim himself can believe in his fate. Many modern voodoo adherents maintain that zombies are merely part of the myth and have never existed in any form, but they remain part of the religion's mysterious past.

Voodoo magic is reputed to be strong enough to kill. One of the most sensationalized features of the religion is the death curse. Cases are on record of people whose death has occurred within days of discovering that they have been cursed. With no apparent physical cause of death, these cases contradict scientific theories of illness in a puzzling way. But researchers have discovered that belief in the effectiveness of any kind of magic greatly enhances its effect. The power of suggestion can be so great that those brought up surrounded by effective use of the supernatural will not question its power. Perfectly healthy people will suffer and even die if they know

Ψ  Ψ

ABOVE: A late 18th-century slave leader, Toussaint L'Ouverture. Like Macandal, he used voodoo as an effective means of stirring rebellion.

themselves to have been the victim of certain types of magic. Anthropologists in the 1940s theorized that the victims of such curses died of sustained shock, while W. Lloyd Warner, pursuing the same problem in the 1960s, suggested that the withdrawal of the community's support, in the knowledge of what was considered a death sentence, contributed to the victim's demise. Members of the victim's group assumed the death to be inevitable and often behaved as if the victim was already dead, beginning funeral preparations and excluding him or her from group activities, including meals. Poisoning cannot be excluded from all of the cases, although most have shown no signs of poison, even after autopsy. Although such cases are tiny in number, they, and the stories of zombies, have done much to inspire fear and fascination.

Followers everywhere accept that in all spirits there is both good and bad, and that their power can be used in either way. Safeguards exist against misuse of voodoo power; such abuse is universally condemned, and it is considered extremely dangerous to manipulate the spirits in order to cause harm. Those tempted to use the power of the invisible against others need to cast their magic carefully; the magic can be countered, and then rebounds upon its sender with more concentrated effect than ever.

Both the African type of voodoo and the Haitian version operate as a supportive set of folk beliefs, but in Haiti more sinister possibilities came to be exploited during the country's turbulent history. During the 1750s a slave named François Macandal, who was a professed sorcerer and generally held to be immortal, escaped. He took cover in the mountains of the north, proclaiming the end of white domination and making it known that voodoo curses had been laid. He then made secret raids on the French-owned plantations. Using his knowledge of medicines he introduced undetectable poisons into the food of plantation owners, causing a wave of fear amongst the settlers and increased confidence among the slaves. Voodoo was seen to be working, and although Macandal was subsequently captured he had planted the seeds for the slave revolts which continued through the rest of the century.

Macandal's interventionist approach continued with Don Juan Felipe Pedro, a Spanish-speaking voodoo priest who influenced some of his followers to develop a more violent and malevolent form of the religion. *Petro* voodoo places more emphasis on death and vengeance, and communicates mainly with the more aggressive *loas*. With its potential for inducing fear it adapted easily to political use, and was employed by most of the political protagonists of the 19th century.

By the beginning of the 20th century Haitian voodoo had become something to be feared as well as respected, and was ripe for misuse. When François Duvalier (better known as "Papa Doc") became President of Haiti in the 1950s, he legalized

Ψ voodoo for the first time and is reputed to have set about exploiting it for his own political purposes. The network of *vodu* temples had been an efficient organization in the days of slavery revolts, and it was not hard for Duvalier to intimidate and control voodoo members through it. Many of the priests worked on his instructions, and those who were loyal to him were rewarded by appointment to government positions. Playing on people's fear of sorcerers and zombies he appointed a kind of secret police with supernatural overtones (the *Tonton Macoute*), and obtained personal details about people which he revealed when apparently possessed by Baron Samedi, one of the most feared of the malevolent *Guedes*. Zombies and death curses were propelled into public consciousness and voodoo acquired an intimidating new dimension which it only began to lose when Duvalier's son and successor, "Baby Doc", was overthrown in 1986.

Since the departure of the Duvaliers the link between voodoo and politics has declined and the threatening overtones which accompanied it have abated. Certainly the followers of the version of voodoo which is being increasingly seen in the United States go to great lengths to deny any malevolence in their religion. Yet even without its more negative elements there is something surprising about voodoo's popularity among middle class Americans. The numbers of adherents are difficult to ascertain because the continuing "Hollywood" image of voodoo makes it a somewhat secretive religion, but American voodoo priests and priestesses believe that no major city is without a voodoo temple, and there are especially large concentrations in New York, Miami, and Los Angeles. American voodoo is an expensive business: the vital ingredients for each ritual must be imported, either from Haiti or directly from Africa, and no initiation, marriage, death, healing, counseling, or magical intervention ceremony can be completed wihout them. Costs for committed believers can rise to thousands of dollars.

Anna Branche is an American who discovered voodoo on holiday in Haiti and became a priestess on her return to the United States. In 1994 she realized her ambition of traveling to West Africa to be initiated as a priestess in the royal court of

ABOVE LEFT: A Haitian Ψ slave revolt, 1791. The inspiration and organizational effectiveness of voodoo helped the slaves in their struggle.

ABOVE: "Papa Doc" Duvalier, who as President of Haiti in the 1950s and 1960s exploited the power of voodoo in order to intimidate his people.

17

RIGHT: Anna Branche, an American whose visit to Haiti changed her life. She discovered voodoo and became a priestess, initiated in both the USA and Benin, West Africa.

BELOW: Preparations for a contemporary Haitian voodoo ceremony include marking these traditional symbols.

Benin. Discussing the appeal of voodoo, she says, "People are practicing voodoo because it works for their needs; it is an earth religion that survives through the hearts and minds of its devotees. We need to go back to our roots, our primitive and natural beginnings . . . people are searching, searching for our salvation, our sanity, our purpose, our mission on this planet." She describes her role as a priestess as "teaching people to recognize themselves and their own powers and their own knowledge and wisdom, in resolving the situations that become traumatic and negative in their lives; to look at things from a spiritual level rather than a mundane, base level ... it is a healing, a natural healing, a physical healing, an emotional healing."

Anna Branche used her experience of Benin to compare Haitian voodoo to its West African roots. She was surprised at the difference, and found that the original version, lacking the Christian accretions that characterized the Haitian form, seemed more closely connected to the earth and its rhythms. "They didn't have to hide it or disguise it. It was real, it was raw, it was pure." But some aspects of the Benin version were a little too raw. The fetish market with its bizarre ingredients, among which were turtles' and dogs' heads, was shocking to Anna and revealed how sanitized United States voodoo had become in order to accommodate American sensibilities. Sacrifice of chickens and occasionally goats is accepted as part of Haitian and American voodoo, but other ritual ingredients tend to be less overtly alarming than those used in Africa.

Anna detected another difference, too: the African emphasis was more firmly on voodoo for the benefit of the group, as opposed to the American focus on self-realization and individual problem-solving. Here is a possible key to voodoo's endurance. Always an empowering religion, it is flexible enough to adapt to the needs of different societies. The spirits are there to be contacted and to supply answers; the questions depend on the preoccupations of each social group. Add to this the sense of mystery and power which surrounds contact with the spirits, and the individual drama of the possession experience, and it is hard to see how such a potent mixture could fail to appeal.

SHAMANISTIC SOCIETIES

Practitioners of voodoo are not alone in their quest to harness the power and wisdom of the spirit world; in most societies and times we can find groups and individuals who want to go beyond the usual constraints and seek transcendent knowledge of the world beyond. In contrast to voodoo, where the spirits possess the humans, shamanism is about the shaman or priest controlling the spirits. A shaman therefore takes the initiative in visiting the spirits in their world, but that world is not easily accessible. Shamanism is an ecstatic experience – the techniques used produce a trance-like state in which, separated from the normal human condition, the shaman can travel in search of knowledge and power. Shamans may sometimes be women, especially older women, but they are generally men; whichever sex they are, they are special people whose particular gifts are supplemented by training. The shaman's chief role is to focus the psychic power of the community onto the positive aims of health, strength, and fertility and the restating of control over the forces of the supernatural. In this way they can influence the outcome of illnesses, wars, and hunting expeditions, all of which they see as controlled by the spirits of this other, parallel reality.

Shamanistic societies are found from Inner Asia and Russia, through Oceania and Indonesia to the Americas, although many of these societies are now in decline. Despite the wide spread of shamanism through quite dissimilar cultures, the practises are usually remarkably similar. Signs of the existence of shamans go back as far as the prehistoric Paleolithic period, where they are linked to the all-important world of the hunt. The walls of the French caves of Les Trois Frères, for example, have 15,000-year-old paintings showing a shaman dancing among the bison with a hunting bow – an image familiar today among shamanistic hunting peoples. In the caves at Lascaux, other Paleolithic wall paintings show entranced shamans with bison. More recent rock carvings in the former USSR, dated 5000 BC, show a shaman dancing with his traditional equipment of mask and drum. In hunting societies the humans are dependent on the animals for their survival and need somehow to be in contact. Shamans are the only beings able to

BELOW: A South Korean shaman dances into an ecstatic trance. Through him, members of his society may make contact with the spirits which influence mortal life.

straddle both worlds, to locate the powers they need and to influence them. Through them the animals may be appeased and controlled, persuaded to give up their lives for the sake of the hunters. As a modern Iglulik Eskimo (Inuit) commented, "The greatest peril of life lies in the fact that human food consists entirely of souls."

Whenever things are going wrong – illness, accident, poor hunting, bad relations with neighbors – the shaman is the person who can put it right. His role is vital in several areas. Illness, for example, is thought in many shamanistic societies to be caused by the loss of the victim's soul, caused by either the spirits or the manipulations of a sorcerer. Only the shaman can locate the soul during his expeditions to the world of the spirits, and arrange for its restoration. Likewise only he is able to find and remove objects which may have entered the victim's body to cause it harm. When he visits the spirit world he can talk to the animal powers to discover the movement of game, persuade game into his group's area, influence weather, and predict future events. Shamans can also uncover lost items, a skill at which many of them excel. These are all services that are needed by everyone, yet inevitably some ambivalence is felt toward the shaman. It is assumed that his intentions are only for good, yet his knowledge and power are so awe-inspiring that he is frequently avoided and has few close friends.

BELOW: This painting of a Siberian shaman shows a close association with the animal world, reflected in the feathered cloak and antler head-dress.

Shamans can demonstrate their powers not only through healing and divination but also through magic. They share the qualities of the spirits; thus they too are impervious to fire and can become invisible and fly through the air, as far as the moon or even out into space. They can overturn the laws of nature, assume the shape of animals, foretell the future – a shaman is the most complete practitioner of the supernatural known to mankind.

The acquiring of this knowledge and its practise are no easy or pleasant matter – shamans are both born *and* made. Potential shamans often reveal their sense of "differentness" during adolescence, when they become solitary and have visions. The Siberian Chukchee people describe a certain look in the eye of young shamans – a far-seeing brightness that indicates a heightened visionary gift. During the period of transition and training, the shaman is effectively remade. During trances he journeys to the spirit world and is destroyed there. The visions and experiences of this time are terrifying. He may be decapitated, dismembered, burned, and generally reduced to a skeleton, his human characteristics erased. Then he is reconstructed by the spirits, his body renewed but altered, his mind strengthened by the tests he has survived. He learns the geography of the spirit world and talks to the dead, and discovers how to move, through ecstatic trance, between the two worlds. There are traditional lore and poetry to learn and magical techniques to perfect. To function successfully, the shaman must know how to negotiate the paths which will deliver him safely to and from the spirit world.

Once shamans learn to move at will into altered states of consciousness they may find the transformation essential to their own wellbeing. Some nonpracticing shamans become uncontroled in their behavior and unable to function in their society. Anthropologists have speculated that shamans are actually or potentially victims of mental illness, which the rigid specifications of the trance training controls. It has been suggested that such societies deal with their mentally unstable undividuals by simply turning them into shamans. Certainly some shamans go through a pre-initiation phase which has much in common with mental illness as defined in Western societies. But such shamans overcome this experience

BELOW: An artist's representation of the inner world of the Siberian shaman.

and use it in some way in their shamanistic training. Fully qualified shamans have complete control over their entry into the trance state and behave normally at other times. Most shamans have been found to be healthy and strong and of above-average intelligence; they are often the most capable members of their age group in their community. Their adventures in the spirit world, far from being aberrant, follow traditionally laid paths and fit into the expectations of their particular society.

Observing shamans has led Westerners to look closely at the nature of different types of experience, and to wonder if the reality into which the mentally ill wander involuntarily may be similar to that which shamans and indeed the many other magical and mystical practitioners through the ages have deliberately sought to enter and control. One interesting point is that shamanistic accounts of the other world are remarkably consistent across cultures, centering on the place of the human world in the universe. Many people believe that what the shamans discover is a part of the human mind that normally remains untapped. Paracelsus, an innovative

Swiss physician and philosopher who believed that we had hardly begun to discover the potential of our minds, wrote in the 16th century: "Everyone may educate and regulate his imagination so as to come thereby into contact with spirits, and be taught by them."

In the words of an elderly Navaho healer, "the most important thing I learned from my grandfathers was that there is a part of the mind that we don't really know about, and that is the part that is most important in whether we become sick or remain well." Shamanistic cures are not satisfactorily explained by Western science, although there are some interesting parallels between shamanistic models of sickness and the most recent medical thinking. Shamans visualize illness as an intrusion, permitted by a loss of personal power, much as doctors now think of illness as a breakdown of immunity. They direct their efforts to discovering the reasons for the weakness, and re-establishing the person's psychic defences. The curing process is often dramatic and expressive, usually involving close family and sometimes featuring the extraction of objects from the victim's body. This apparently miraculous surgery is generally accepted to be an element of conjuring which seems to increase the success of the cure; shamans explain that the deception is necessary to demonstrate to the victim something which is otherwise beyond their understanding.

Seances are held regularly in shamanistic societies, and are attended by all those with an interest to pursue, whether in healing or in advice. They vary in detail according to each society, but there are broad similarities in the drums, drugs, dancing, songs and poetry which herald the shaman's journey to the spirit world. Many seances are theatrical occasions with social as well as spiritual aspects. Inuit seances give opportunities for people to confess their transgressions and for the whole group to unite in a tension-releasing burst of semi-trance excitement. At some, strange magical events occur. In 1879 Cecil Denny, a young member of the Royal Canadian Mounted Police, reported witnessing the violent shaking of a large, heavy Native American tepee, apparently solely upon the will of the entranced shaman. The tepee was resistant to the strongest winds and no one could be seen to be in contact with it, yet it rocked and rose dramatically. In Siberia, some years later, Russian investigators could find no explanation for objects flying through the air during seances, nor could they detect any source for the unnerving spirit voices which punctuated the ceremony.

BELOW: A Yurok shaman of northern California, pictured in the early 20th century, with traditional clothing and drum.

SPIRITUALISM IN THE WEST

During their seances shamans seek to influence the spirits, but there is little thought of personal communication. The spirits are not closely identified with dead personalities, and a shamanistic society's concern is more with the impact of the spirit world on humans than with the fate of the spirits themselves. Some members of other societies have a more personal interest in individual spirits, and are eager to contact them in their life beyond the grave.

During the 19th century, Western Europe and America became gripped by an intense interest in contacting the spirits of the dead. It was not generally believed that the spirit world had power over human life, but it had long been accepted that the dead could appear in the shape of ghosts. In earlier centuries the apparitions came and went as they chose. Usually they were unwelcome and disturbing to those who saw or heard them, and there was little in the way of communication. Typical of traditional silent hauntings is the Grey Lady of Sawston Hall, Cambridge, England. This house, the ancestral home of the Huddleston family, had been a retreat for Mary Tudor in the days before she became Queen in 1553. After narrowly escaping an assassination attempt which ended in the Hall being destroyed by fire, Mary had the house rebuilt for the Huddlestons. After her death in 1558 her ghost began to appear there, wandering through the grounds and entering her former bedroom during the night. But the presence of such apparitions did not prompt the living to go in search of the dead.

All this began to change when, in the middle of the 19th century, the idea of actually talking to the spirits of the dead took hold. This was not an entirely new idea. As early as 1762 a house in London was disturbed by a series of raps and noises. A simple code revealed that the raps were coming from the spirit of Fanny Kent, who had recently died. The spirit went on to accuse her husband of murdering her, leading to a major inquiry. Although the case turned out to be a more earthly conspiracy, the notion that conversation was possible was clearly in existence.

The crucial development was the case of the Fox family, of Hydesville, New York. They started to experience rapping noises in 1848, after they had moved to a new house, and the children, two sisters, discovered that the rappings responded to first clapping and later questions of their own. Thus through a code of raps they were able to get answers to a series of questions which indicated that the rapper was a peddler who had been murdered and unceremoniously buried under the house. Later excavations proved that there was indeed a skeleton and a peddler's tin buried beneath the cellar and walls. The events attracted great publicity and the disruptions caused by the rappings increased. Eventually the Fox sisters left the house and went to live, separately, with other members of their family. The noises in the house did not cease, however, but were overshadowed by further spirit activity which followed the Fox sisters. Soon they began to hold seances in which they received spirit messages, accompanied by table-rocking and other manifestations which were to become standard in the thousands of seances which swept North America and Europe in the following years.

The publicity surrounding the Fox sisters, who, with their married elder sister, later became mediums, led to a great enthusiasm for seances and table-rapping, and

RIGHT: Kate Fox, one of three sisters whose gifts as mediums first appeared in childhood. The events in the family home in Hydesville, New York, sparked the Spiritualist movement.

numbers of other mediums surfaced to supply the demand. Groups were formed and a new movement, Spiritualism, grew up. Spiritualists believed that the rappings, moving objects, and disembodied voices of the seance were proof that it was possible to communicate with those who had died, or "passed over," as they preferred to say. The popularity of seances grew, partly from natural curiosity, but also from the grief of the bereaved and their desire to satisfy themselves that their loved ones lived on in some form. A typical seance would include messages from those "on the other side," reassuring their friends and relatives.

As the movement gathered momentum seances became more dramatic, and sceptics clamored for proof that the phenomena were really supernatural. Believers were not troubled by doubts, and remained unperturbed by the various scandals that erupted. The Fox sisters were said to have confessed to fraud several times; at one point one of them stated that the rappings which started it all had been faked, and that the sounds were actually produced by the girls cracking their knee and toe joints. But many of those who had heard the rappings doubted that this could have been true – it could not have explained the range of sounds, their volume, or the fact that they came from different directions and areas of the room. The sisters experienced financial difficulties in their later years and later retracted their confession, alleging that it had been made for payment. The incident damaged their personal credibility but did little to slow the progress of the Spiritualist movement. As the "psychic cloud" spread, thousands of ordinary men and women took part in seances in which increasingly extraordinary events occurred.

Such was the general eagerness to believe in the phenomena that extraordinarily crude frauds were accepted by many people. It is hard for us now, used to sophisticated laser technology and familiar with illusions in which entire landmarks disappear, to look at photographs of spirit manifestations and believe that intelligent, educated people of the day could have taken them seriously. A particularly blatant example was the "ectoplasm" produced by many mediums during their seances. This opaque, semi-solid substance, supposedly of supernatural origin, was produced by the medium under trance from various bodily apertures. It would then sometimes mould itself into a spirit form. These manifestations were usually accepted at face value by the amazed seance audience, but surviving photographs indicate that considerable suspension of disbelief would often have been necessary. Close attention by investigators revealed cases in which the ectoplasm turned out to be muslin, chewed-up paper, gelatine, or egg white, and as observations became more attentive ectoplasm became less and less a feature of seances. Some ectoplasm sightings did defy explanation, but whether they were especially skilled illusions or true manifes-

LEFT: In the late
1800s, parlour seances
were common at social
gatherings, appealing
to sceptics and
believers alike.

tations cannot now be established. In 1905 a physical medium, Marthe Béraud, was closely studied after claims that she produced ectoplasmic figures; four years of testing failed to discover any trickery.

There is no doubt that, in the general craze, fraud became a major feature of seances. People went to them in order to be thrilled and to witness something extraordinary, and the mediums were under constant pressure to perform. Seances were often held in darkness, with the medium in a curtained-off "cabinet," so there were considerable opportunities for deception. But it would be unwise to assume that mediums who were caught cheating relied upon deception in all their work. Some confessed to occasional trickery but maintained that they only resorted to it when their supernatural gifts were unreliable. They blamed the pressure put upon them to deliver phenomena at every seance, which they found difficult to achieve. Others used tricks in much the same way as a farmer puts china eggs in a hen's nest – real eggs tend to follow. This theory fits with the stories told by many straightforward magicians – that sometimes a trick has taken an unexpected turn which they are quite unable to explain.

Contemporary reports show that mediums were aware that audiences contained some committed believers, some curious but sympathetically minded spectators, and

TOP: Some mediums specialized in producing spirit photographs. This one shows the spirit of Lord Combermere, apparently sitting in his favorite chair.

ABOVE: The Italian medium Linda Gazzera, with an ectoplasmic spirit which convinced witnesses in 1909. They declared fraud to have been out of the question.

a few sceptics. Many followers, in need of reassurance about their dead loved ones and longing for the comfort of a guaranteed afterlife, needed little convincing; but there were others who refused to contemplate the reality of communications from the spirits of the dead. There was firm, sometimes violent opposition to the new movement, both from organized religions and from those who felt that the claims must be simple fraud. Time and energy were devoted to attempts to prove or disprove the authenticity of seances. Some mediums could be dismissed quite rapidly: along with muslin "ectoplasm," false "spirit hands," and pre-written "spirit messages" were found. A British medium, Francis Ward Monck, was found guilty of fraud and sentenced to three months in prison in 1876. Another medium, the American Henry Slade, well known and previously tested with complete success, was detected in trickery and also sentenced to prison in the same year. Despite the obvious deceptions, both were vigorously defended by witnesses who claimed to have seen previous incontrovertible proof of the their powers. The outcome of these cases made the sceptics triumphant, and jokes were made at the spiritualists' expense, but many cases remained which could not be so easily refuted.

One such was Daniel Dunglas Home, a medium who consistently performed a wide range of extraordinary acts, empowered, as he insisted, by spirit forces. Born in Scotland in 1883, he grew up in the care of an aunt in Connecticut, USA, exhibiting signs of clairvoyance and powers of healing from childhood. Early tests by William Bryant and David Wells of Harvard University established Home as an impressive medium. He readily admitted that fraud was rampant in the world of spiritualism and was vituperative in his condemnation of those who brought the subject into disrepute. He commented that "between spiritualism and the majority of the abuses by which it is disgraced there is just as little in common as between a precious stone and the mud which may happen to cling to it."

Home's actions were observed by hundreds of witnesses, who were forced by the evidence of their eyes to believe in their authenticity; exhaustive tests and safeguards failed to reveal any trace of trickery. He had experienced paranormal incidents since childhood and had precognition of his mother's death. Later he began to communicate with her spirit and then those of others. Gradually his mediumship powers grew until he was able to use the power of the spirits to perform extraordinary feats, including table-moving, the manifestation of hands and, most disturbing, the levitation and elongation of his own body. All of these feats were performed anywhere that he was asked, in good light, without the use of a cabinet or curtain and in close proximity to any number of witnesses. He was seen to rise unsupported to the ceiling, and even to float in and out of a window, and witnesses describe with incredulity how his height could contract and elongate in front of their eyes, stretching to a measured 7 ft (over 2 m) on one occasion.

He was closely studied, especially by Sir William Crookes, a renowned scientist and Fellow of the Royal Society in London, whose increasingly stringent conditions left no room for maneuver. Witnesses from all walks of life were overwhelmed by the experience. Each scientific investigation came to the same conclusion, but all that could be said definitively was that the events had occurred and that no artificial means could be detected. Those who had not witnessed Home were sceptical when the events were described, much to the frustration of those who had been present. Some witnesses were unable afterward to believe what they had seen, and returned to prove to themselves that it was all deception. No one was ever able to do so.

Spiritualism had caught the attention of many of the eminent scientists and thinkers of the day, who were understandably curious and eager to apply their scientific method to such radical challenges. One of the first was Dr Alfred Russel Wallace, who had worked with Charles Darwin on the development of his theory of evolution. Wallace set out to test the honesty of a succession of mediums, including Agnes Nichol, later Mrs Guppy, who called upon the spirits of the dead to furnish various proofs of their existence, including levitations of objects and "apports" – objects brought directly from the spirit world. During seances Agnes Nichol could produce,

RIGHT: Henry Slade, one of two mediums convicted of fraud in 1876. Many witnesses were prepared to swear that they had previously seen him perform in fraud-proof conditions, and their support for him continued.

BELOW: Daniel Dunglas Home, possibly the most dramatic and convincing of the early 20th-century mediums. This shows a famous event, in which he was seen to float in and out of an upper window of a house in London.

BELOW: Salon seances were the height of fashion at the end of the 19th century. Moving tables and loud rapping noises provoked a combination of consternation and thrilled delight in the participants.

apparently from nowhere, large bouquets of flawless exotic flowers, covered in fine, cold dew. To remove any doubts, the audience could request the type of flowers, which would then materialize, rapidly, to order. This was done in Wallace's own home, where the possibility of false floors or ceilings was discounted, and where there was no opportunity to conceal the flowers. For this, and the rappings and levitations which occurred during the seances, Wallace could find no explanation, despite his most ingenious investigations.

Wallace was joined in his researches by other respected British scientists. Three physicists, Sir William Crookes, Sir William Barrett, and Sir Oliver Lodge, were amongst those determined to test the mediums' claims. Although they did detect frauds, all of them encountered some phenomena which they could not explain by any means known to them. In 1882 Barrett was instrumental in setting up the Society for Psychical Research (SPR), an organization which to this day conducts research into supernatural phenomena. During its years of existence the Society has recorded numerous unexplained cases, but scientists not directly involved have been reluctant to accept these experiences as proof.

Sir Oliver Lodge was neutral on the subject until asked to conduct some tests for the SPR. Some of these involved the American medium Leonora Piper, who specialized in direct communication with the dead. She had an ability to provide accurate private information about a wide variety of subjects which stunned Lodge, and indeed, all the other investigators who spent years laying traps for her. Detectives were hired to see if she was researching her potential subjects, but she was never discovered to

LEFT: Many mediums "apported" objects from the spirit world. These flowers appeared during a seance, apparently out of thin air.

RIGHT: Sir Oliver Lodge, one of several eminent scientists called in to test the claims of spiritualist mediums. Their investigations were rigorous, and fraud was often detected. Despite this, their scepticism was sometimes overcome by events they could not explain.

BELOW : Mrs Leonora Piper, who specialized in supplying complete strangers with accurate messages from their deceased relatives. Sir Oliver Lodge applied his most sophisticated tests to her but was never able to detect fraud.

Ψ

be in contact with anyone who could have furnished her with the details she produced. Unknown and unexpected sitters did not disturb her; she could still give them unsettlingly accurate information about their deceased relatives. Often these communications came in the voice of the deceased, to the shock and consternation of the sitters.

Investigators attempted to explain this uncanny accuracy as more to do with telepathy or thought-reading than communication with the dead, a theory frequently offered to explain the success of mediums. Against this was the fact that some of the details were unknown to the sitters themselves and were only found to be correct on later consultation with relatives. Lodge, for example, had received a watch in the post one morning. He produced it at the seance that evening, when Mrs Piper identified the relative who had previously owned it and described in detail events from the childhood of the deceased man and his brother. Some of this was meaningless to Lodge, but was later confirmed by the surviving brother.

Ψ

Throughout the years of its popularity researchers into spiritualism were confronted with a dilemma. Successions of eminent scientists and thinking individuals found themselves faced by things which they knew were physically impossible; yet they had seen and felt for themselves that these things *had* indeed happened. They could only conclude that the mediums' claims must be true. But only experience could bring conviction, and the investigators' conclusions counted for nothing with their colleagues. The afterlife remained as much a mystery as ever.

Clear proof would be an unambiguous message from a deceased person who has announced this intention before death, but there are logical problems. If a copy of the message is left as a check, its very existence means that human interference or telepathy can be cited. The nearest that investigators have come to proof is a series of apparently coded messages which seemed to have been sent by deceased members of the Society for Psychical Research. Frederic W. H. Myers, a founder member of the Society, had always said that he would try to send back a message if, indeed, the afterlife existed, and his colleagues Edmund Gurney and Henry Sidgwick were equally prepared to try.

BELOW: Frederic W. H. Myers, President of the Society for Psychical Research. His determination to communicate from beyond the grave may be the answer to the "cross correspondences," coded messages received after his death.

Myers had never said what form his message would take, but shortly after his death a medium friend, Mrs Verrall, began to receive messages from a spirit called Myers. Her daughter also received the messages, as did the medium Leonora Piper and another, the sister of the British writer Rudyard Kipling, in India. All the messages were in the form of automatic writing, and included instructions for sending them back to Mrs Verrall. Other mediums became involved as time went on. The Society for Psychical Research analyzed the messages, which ran into thousands of pages, over 30 years. They discovered many similarities and cross-references between the sources, which were rich in literary

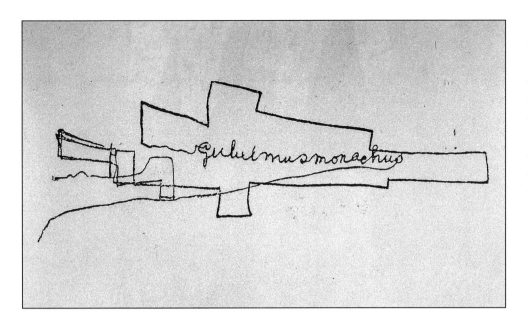

LEFT: An example of
automatic writing
from the early 20th
century. During
seances the mediums
produce messages in a
script unlike their
own, often with closed
eyes or in a darkened
room.

allusion and almost amounted to a code. Collusion between the mediums was ruled out, and the sheer volume of the correspondence over such a period made coincidence virtually impossible.

Automatic writing played a vital role in the transmission of these messages, and it is equally important in other areas of communication with spirits. Whilst in a trance, a medium will start to write, often with the pen loosely held and sometimes with closed eyes. The writing is usually unlike the medium's own, and the style often dramatically different. It may claim to come from an unknown dead person, or from a famous one. A startling feature of such writings is that they are fluent and rapid, unlike the uneven progress of most literary effort. Pearl Curran, an American housewife in St Louis, began to experiment with a friend's ouija board (an alphabet and sensitive pointer through which sentences can be spelt out) in 1913. Without her conscious influence the board began to spell out a message from a spirit contact called Patience Worth. This spirit went on to communicate over a million words of poetry, plays and novels to Pearl over a period of years. Patience claimed to have lived in the 17th century, and her work was filled with historical detail, not just of that period, but of later ones too. Pearl herself was ignorant of and uninterested in history, and consciously knew nothing of the subjects about which Patience wrote through her. In addition she had no interest in literature or books and had never attempted any form of creative writing before her first seance. Yet the works of Patience are of high literary quality and were successfully published without reference to their unusual provenance. It could be said that Patience represented a side of Pearl's personality which was somehow denied expression, but this does not explain the wealth of knowledge which the works reflect, or the uncanny speed with which the edited texts emerged from the medium's hand.

Equally mysterious is the case of Rosemary Brown, who began, in 1964, to receive messages from the spirit of the 19th-century composer Franz Liszt. Then she began to write out music dictated to her by Liszt, Chopin, Beethoven, and others. Rosemary herself played the piano, but only at an elementary level. The music she

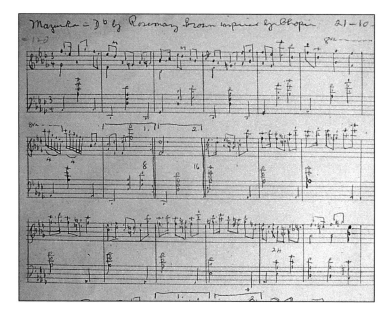

Ψ ABOVE: **Rosemary Brown** and part of the fluently written manuscript of a mazurka communicated by Chopin.

wrote, however, was often complex in form and included orchestration. Typically, it was written with speed and fluency, just like dictation. The music, analyzed by prominent modern musicians, is written very closely and recognizably in the style of the spirit composers and could easily have been attributed to them if it had been found at the back of a cupboard. Most agree, however, that it is not comparable to their best compositions; it tends to typify early, younger work. Sceptics then argue that it seems unlikely that spirits would bother to transmit music less developed than the compositions they were achieving at the time of their death, and a more reasonable explanation is that Rosemary has a rare musical talent of which she is consciously unaware. The same counter-arguments apply – where are the years of training needed to produce music at this level, or even to write it out correctly? The skills involved in even transcribing orchestral music, let alone composing it, are considerable; given the speed with which the operation occurs, and the sheer bulk of music produced, this makes the unconscious talent explanation unlikely. Spiritualists often encounter a problem with the quality of spirit communications. Their view is that spirits are no longer involved with worldly matters and are therefore less concerned with the detail of their messages. Their point is to demonstrate that such contact is possible, and we should accept the messages for the fact, not the quality, of their existence.

Similar arguments apply to the artistic efforts of the British psychic Matthew Manning, who during the 1970s began to produce, rapidly and without preliminary sketches, paintings in the style of dead artists such as Aubrey Beardsley and Pablo Picasso. Manning had experienced paranormal manifestations since childhood, and explained that as he concentrated his thoughts upon the artist his hands would involuntarily move across the paper. Again, many of his paintings do not measure up to the best work of the artists concerned, but there is no obvious explanation for their spontaneous appearance. Even more bizarre is the work of the Brazilian Luiz Gasparetto, who during the 1970s began producing pictures emanating from artists including Renoir and Cézanne. Not only are the paintings confidently in the style of each artist, but Gasparetto produces them in semi-darkness, in a trance state, and at enormous speed. He is even able to paint two pictures at once, using both hands, as if his body is simply the agent through which the picture is produced.

These cases of automatic writing and artistic activity have all taken place in the 20th century, at a time when spiritualist activity, at least in a domestic setting, has generally decreased. The craze for home seances had worn off by the start of World War II, but serious mediums continued to work. They are now subject to sophisticated tests, and face audiences

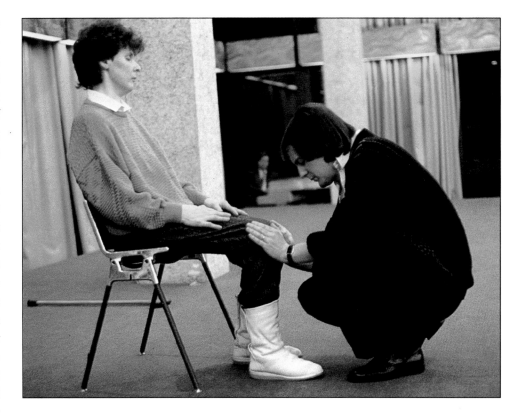

who are less easily convinced than their Victorian counterparts. Physical manifestations no longer play much of a part, but the emphasis on communication with the dead has, if anything, increased.

Probably one of the best-known 20th-century mediums was the British Doris Stokes, who died in 1987. She became aware of her ability to operate on a paranormal level during her youth, but was married and a mother before she received her first message from the world beyond death. Her father, who had died many years before, appeared to her and told her of two crucial events in her life, both of which subsequently occurred. She began to develop her talent by attending seances, and discovered an easy-going style of conversing with the dead. Her undramatic, nontrance-like delivery of messages could not be further from the thrills and excitement of the Victorian seance, yet the atmosphere was often charged with emotion. Doris Stokes's success lay in her ability to deliver, repeatedly, accurate details which identified the deceased beyond doubt to their living relatives. There is a wealth of testimony to her ability to give accurate messages to people whose background she could not have known. It has been observed that the information was usually already known to the sitter; this suggests, again, that the medium's talents may have lain less in contacting the dead than in reading the minds of the sitters. Doris Stokes vehemently denied this and maintained her certainty that the information came from beyond the grave, but it is possible that she was not consciously aware of the process taking place. She admitted to occasional cheating, especially later in her career, saying that the pressure forced her to produce results of some sort. She pointed out, however, that these could be easily spotted as they were much inferior to "the real thing."

ABOVE: Matthew Manning is best known as a medium for the work of deceased 19th- and 20th-century artists. However, he has other psychic gifts, and is shown here demonstrating his powers as a healer.

Ψ

Ψ

LEFT: This painting, in the style of Modigliani, was executed by the Brazilian Luiz Gasparetto during a seance. Painting rapidly and without corrections, he claims to be merely the agent of the spirit artist.

CHANNELERS

Through television, Doris Stokes brought spiritualism to an internationally wide modern audience, but since her death spiritualist mediums have assumed a less public profile. Their place in media consciousness was taken during the 1970s and 1980s by channelers – mediums who communicate with various classes of nonphysical beings, including angels, spirits , and even extraterrestrial life forms. Channeling tends to be less personal than spiritualism, and the spirits select themselves rather than being approached by the channeler. The messages are of more general importance – the difference between reassurance for the bereaved and the transmission of vital knowledge from representatives of the spirit world. Channeling first came into prominence with the publication, during the late 1960s and early 1970s, of books written by the American channeler Jane Roberts. She had been channeling a multidimensional being known as Seth, who in twice-weekly sessions in her home revealed the existence of parallel realities. He maintained that these other realities were available to humans, and that the only limitations on human experience were self-imposed. After Jane's death in 1984, other channelers claimed to have been contacted by Seth in order to resume his communication with our world. The best-known channeler is probably the Californian Kevin Ryerson, who channeled messages for the actress Shirley MacLaine during the 1980s. He appeared in a television series which chronicled MacLaine's search for spiritual enlightment, and was seen in the process of channeling messages from some of his spirit beings.

BELOW: The 1970s and 1980s saw a growth of cults in which believers attempted to get in touch with higher beings.

Although there are superficial resemblances, channeling has more in common with shamanism than spiritualism, emphasizing the power of the supernatural world and the necessity of our being able to gain access to it. While not all of their messages imply that they have achieved contact with a higher wisdom, many channelers genuinely see these attempts as the only hope for a solution to humanity's problems. In this respect they are part of one of mankind's most ancient and enduring quests, to reach past our limited world of time and space to the spirit world beyond.

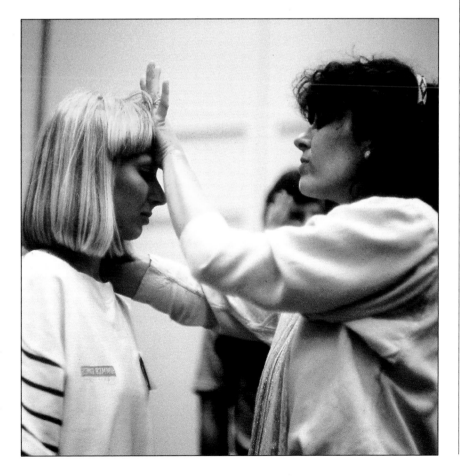

CHAPTER II

DOING THE IMPOSSIBLE

ABOVE: Angels were a favorite subject for medieval artists. This French 13th-century illumination shows them at a traditional task, playing their harps.

Wander into any book or stationery shop in Europe or America during the 1990s and you are likely to find yourself surrounded by angels. Their calm and beautiful faces regard you from greeting cards, wrapping paper, posters, and book covers. Artists through the ages have been inspired by the idea of these winged emissaries of the divine, but it is puzzling to see the obvious popularity of these images in contemporary secular society. It seems even more perplexing to turn on the radio and television and listen to first-hand accounts of encounters between ordinary people and what was considered, in popular culture at least, to be an extinct species.

ENCOUNTERS WITH ANGELS

It seems that angelic sightings are not particularly rare. In the recent past, those who experienced them were reluctant to publicize the fact; they feared mockery or misunderstanding, and wished to keep the experience personal. But once a few accounts had emerged to a positive reception in the media during the 1980s and 1990s, people overcame their reservations and accounts of angel encounters began to flow. Hope Price, a British author who in 1993 published a collection of stories, entitled simply *Angels*, estimates that there are hundreds, possibly thousands, of people alive in Britain today who have seen angels. These figures are echoed by stories emerging on other continents, demonstrating similarly high instances of angel awareness.

A typical angel encounter described by Hope Price involved a decidedly nontraditional angel plumber. A single mother living in Yorkshire was very worried because her gas boiler had broken down and she did not have enough money to have it

ABOVE: Angels were not limited to the Judeo-Christian tradition. Here a late 16th-century embroidery shows an Indian image derived from Persia.

RIGHT: Fra Angelico's angel, richly serene and sumptuously winged, typifies an image which has endured for centuries, bringing comfort and inspiration to successive generations.

LEFT: This modern representation reflects the renewed presence of angels in our consciousness. Modern angels often retain their wings, and, in this instance, their lutes.

Ψ

put right. As she was contemplating her plight, coping with small children in a house without heating or hot water, her doorbell rang and a plumber announced that he had come to repair her boiler. When she asked him how much it would cost, he said there was no charge. After doing the work he left the house and disappeared, although there were no cars or people in sight. The woman, who had previously told no one of her plight, realized that her plumber was in fact an angel – sent, she believed, in response to her desperate prayer.

Other accounts include the story of a runaway farm tractor, heading downhill towards a car park full of picnicking holidaymakers. Horrified bystanders saw its driver wrestling to control the huge machine; he finally succeeded in diverting it from the car park but, as a consequence, both tractor and driver plunged over the adjacent cliff edge. Witnesses then discovered that the tractor had rolled away while unattended, and that amongst its wreckage there was no sign of a body or any other trace of the man they had seen diverting it from its collision course.

Countless other examples exist: angels appear in human form to perform tasks both extraordinary and minor, and in more recognizable form, such as the huge winged angel which a Londoner remembers hovering protectively over his house during one of the worst nights of the World War II Blitz. Traditional angels, winged and clothed in white and gold, seem to appear most commonly to children, or at the time of death.

Even in secular times the characteristics of angels are well understood. This is not surprising when we consider the near universality of angels in human culture and history. Derived from the Greek word for "messenger," the term "angel" means an agent or servant of divine power, a spiritual being who travels between the realms of the sublime and the earthly. They exist outside natural laws, so can easily perform miraculous acts. They are known in Judaism, Christianity, Zoroastrianism, and Islam, with comparable concepts in Hindu and Buddhist teaching. Images of angels appear in classical times, and as far afield as Bali and Scandinavia. They are not divine themselves, and can be both tempted and corrupted. In the Judeo-Christian tradition fallen angels became Lucifer, the Devil, and his demons, but true angels represent purity and kindness. They are one of the most comforting and appealing notions in religious history, and appear in art, music, and literature throughout the ages.

Ψ

Angels are often found delivering divine messages, usually vital ones with profound effects. They are frequently the heralds of new religions; it was the angel Gabriel who told Muhammad that he was the prophet of God and dictated to him the Koran; an angel who came to the Persian prophet

ABOVE: The angel Gabriel, bringing the Virgin Mary the message of the forthcoming birth of her son, Jesus.

Zoroaster and prompted the beginning of Zoroastrianism; and an angel who told the Virgin Mary that she would give birth to her son. More often, angels come to help humans; they comfort and protect. There is a subdivision of guardian angels whose role is to watch over individuals, and angels can be summoned by prayer, as the angel plumber was, to bring assistance. Scholars throughout history have devoted themselves to the study of angels, their nature, habits, numbers, and characteristics. In the 2nd century, the Chronicles of Enoch named and described hundreds of angels, and during the early years of Christianity speculation became intense, culminating in the elaborate works of European theologians in the late Middle Ages. Heaven was considered to be an ordered hierarchy, with nine choirs of angels circulating around the Throne of Glory. The choirs were crowned by the highest order, the seraphim; below them, in order of status, came the cherubim, the thrones, the dominations, the virtues, the powers, the principalities, the archangels, and the common, everyday angels. The higher choirs communicated only with God and each other, while the lower ones communicated the divine illumination to mortals. The only angels which mortals met were thus the lowliest and least perfect, which theologians felt might account for their occasional eccentricities.

The problems faced by the Church during the 14th century, including the rise of heresy and the remorseless progress of the Black Death across Europe, diverted ecclesiastical interest. The attention previously given to the heavenly hosts was directed instead to the minute study of the devils and demons who seemed to be causing so much trouble. As Church interest in angels waned, so did popular attention, leaving them largely to artists and writers.

Angels continued to be seen, however, mostly by the devout and virtuous – for whom their appearance was sometimes taken as evidence of saintliness. Certain angels were witnessed by more than one person, and occasionally by large numbers. In August 1914, at the start of World War I, the Allied armies in Mons, Belgium, found themselves close to defeat by the Germans; there was nothing to protect their outnumbered ranks from annihilation. Then, quite suddenly, the German cavalry stopped and turned. Their horses were seen to refuse to go forward, and many of the

Ψ ABOVE: A 13th-century Bohemian demon, a fallen angel in opposition to the heavenly variety.

RIGHT: A sheet music illustration from 1915, showing how the extraordinary events at Mons, passing by word of mouth, soon sparked the public imagination.

men simply turned and retreated. These respites allowed the Allied armies to regroup and find new defensive positions. Numerous eye-witness accounts from both sides of the battle describe the sudden appearance of groups of angels, hovering in the sky between the two armies. Some German reports spoke of an overwhelming feeling that they could not go forward, while others described seeing huge troop reinforcements which convinced them that they could not continue. An inexplicable event had occurred. Undoubtedly many lives had been saved, but it is hard to guess why angels should have intervened in this battle and not in other bloodbaths. For every account of angels saving and preserving life, there are clearly thousands of instances when atrocities have not been prevented, and this raises a central question about angel activity: if angels can help a desperate mother, protect a house from bombs, or scoop a child from the path of oncoming traffic, why do they not do so all the time? Although many of those helped by angels have been pious individuals who have prayed for help, others were without religious conviction and were astounded by the intervention. And very many prayers from devout people have gone unanswered.

Despite these difficulties, the central role played by angels in human life shows little sign of diminishing, partly because of the powerful impact which the encounters produce. Witnesses experience feelings of joy and revelation which they claim affect the rest of their lives. Stories of the encounters give pleasure to many who would claim no religious belief; it is comforting to us all to think that there may indeed be angels hovering at our door, rather than the violence and hopelessness all too commonly found in contemporary society.

PROPHETS

Angels may be miracle workers, but they are not alone in this. The divinities of major world religions naturally embody supreme power, which can, on occasion, be delegated to mortals. Most gods and goddesses represent the pinnacle of moral perfection, and it is this extreme virtue which is one of the sources of their power. Mortals who are virtuous, pious and faithful can theoretically also be capable of miraculous events, either as agents of a divinity or by reason of their own piety.

Judeo-Christian religions provide many examples of natural laws suspended or overturned by the power of virtue. The Old Testament emphasizes miracles as part of a broader plan to convince the world that there is only *one* God, and that His power is infinite. The power of the supernatural is on the side of the righteous – those who believe. It protects them, as the Israelites were protected by

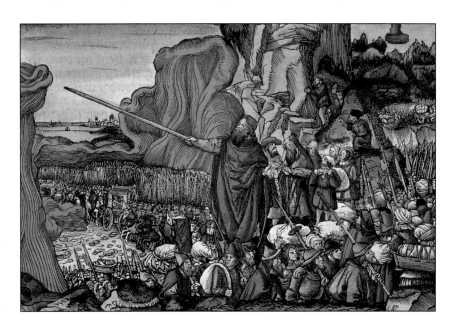

BELOW: A woodcut from the Luther Bible shows an Old Testament miracle: Moses rescuing his followers from a pursuing army by dividing the Red Sea.

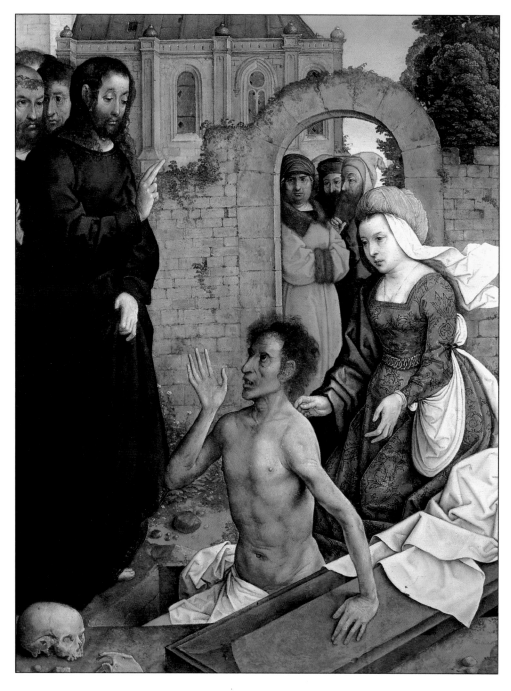

Ψ RIGHT: Jesus Christ was the most consistent miracle-worker ever known. This 15th-century painting shows one of his most dramatic acts, the raising of Lazarus from the dead.

the parting of the Red Sea; it provides for them, as when the Israelites discovered manna to eat in the wilderness; and it smites their enemies.

It was essential to prove this point, not only to the Children of Israel but also to their enemies. The prophet Moses was God's mouthpiece, and led his chosen people into the promised land; he performed miracles as God's agent, using his delegated powers both to reveal God's will and to execute it. Through him came a constant stream of communications, including detailed instructions. The most central of these are the Ten Commandments, which have been the cornerstone of Judeo-Christian notions of right and wrong for thousands of years. Miraculously written on tablets of stone, they were brought down by Moses from Mount Sinai as God's actual words – the essential moral code of His people. All the Old Testament miracles have a serious function – they are never for worldly ends or to satisfy personal desires. They demonstrate God's credentials and use His authority to build up new standards of spiritual and social behaviour.

Other Old Testament prophets were provided with special powers to underline the point that the righteous could do things which ordinary mortals could not. When, as recorded in Chapter 3 of the Book of Daniel, Shadrach, Mesach and Abednego refused to deny their God, they were thrust into the pagan Babylonian King Nebuchadnezzar's fiery furnace. The heat was so intense that the guards ordered to throw them in were killed instantly. Yet witnesses, including leading members of Nebuchadnezzar's government, saw the three chosen of God walk, not only unharmed but totally unaffected, from the flames. They did not even smell of the fire afterwards.

New Testament miracles spell out even more clearly the connection between divinity and power. The identity of Jesus Christ as the Son of God (the God of the Jews, whose followers had, as a result of the events of the Old Testament, become the first monotheistic religious group) is established through a string of miracles, beginning with the Virgin Birth and culminating in the Resurrection – triumph over death itself. Each of the minor miracles has its place in Christ's teaching, underlining the new morality of unselfish love. Many of the miracles which Jesus himself performed, including healing the sick, turning water into wine, and walking on water, have reportedly been performed by others; but, together with the unsurpassed events of his birth and death, they have inspired one of the world's most extensive religions for 2,000 years.

SUFIS, DERVISHES, AND SADHUS

The religion of Islam allows the existence of miracles, but makes little use of them. Muhammad did not perform them, but some Islamic holy men are known to possess considerable powers, including ones which are apparently miraculous. Some members of Islamic societies wish to have a closer experience of divinity than is possible through the normal practise of their religion. In this they follow the Sufis, who were the mystically inclined devotees of early Islam, and who sought ways of approaching God more directly.

The techniques which they developed are still practiced by specialized orders known as dervishes. Each order makes use of particular techniques to help them achieve unity with God, which successful adherents claim to do in periods of religious ecstasy. Paradoxically, this most personal experience is achieved only through denial of the self, a skill which initiates acquire through lengthy training. Such techniques are not easily learned and demand years of dedication, loyalty, discipline, and total obedience both to the leader and to the inflexible rules of the sect. There is no easy way to reach the state of understanding and knowledge which dervishes seek, and initiates, now declining in numbers, enter a hard and remorselessly demanding life.

Ψ ABOVE: A group of
Moulavi dervishes,
performing their
whirling ritual.

The best-known order is the Moulavi or Mevleviya group, more popularly known as the whirling dervishes. Founded in the 13th century, they base their ideas on the teachings of the Persian poet Jalal al-Din Rumi. The Moulavi enter their ecstatic seance during a hypnotic, twirling dance, and have become familiar to Westerners as one of the few dervish sects to have been seen outside their normal religious setting. The smooth, seemingly endless dance has symbolic power as well as being a route to the "forgetting" of individual identity that is necessary to enter the divine experience.

Other dervishes use quite different techniques. The Chishti lead a wandering existence in India, and use music in their rituals. In stark contrast the Qadiri, who can be found from India to Ethiopia, specialize in extreme acts of violence on their own bodies. These dervishes push swords and skewers through their flesh, handle burning coals and red-hot metal, eat glass, and handle poisonous snakes. They do not object to witnesses being present, and observers have seen dervishes mutilate themselves without bleeding, blistering, or any other appearance of suffering or injury. Rhythmic chanting and breathing methods produce an altered state in which the dervishes are able to perform these acts which would be intolerably painful in other circumstances. They do not, strictly speaking, enter a trance, as they are perfectly aware of their surroundings and respond normally to conversation. Western doctors have been unable to explain or understand the process. The Qadiri believe that their faith and the level of spiritual awareness which they have developed protect them during the time that they make the mystic journey out of themselves. They view their actions as evidence of the strength of their faith and the depth of their religious experience, and dervishes seek more extreme acts as they feel increasingly empowered. For these individuals, this public demonstration is the pinnacle of their training, the tangible sign that they have transcended the usual operation of natural laws.

Other Eastern spiritual traditions are rich in stories of miracle workers. The ability to defy certain natural laws is almost commonplace amongst the leading exponents of religions such as Buddhism, where the mastery of these powers, including control over the human body as well as the ability to influence events outside it, is considered to be part of spiritual training. Such powers are believed to come through spiritual purification and discipline, and are essential to the achievement of an advanced spiritual position. Miracles such as levitation and translocation are easily performed by the masters of such purity, but the actual enactment of them is not always considered appropriate. Buddha strongly discouraged his followers from miracle-working, although Buddhist writings contain many accounts of him performing them himself. Routine miracle-working can overindulge the ego of even the most spiritually heightened individuals and cause them to be diverted from the religious path – a reminder that power leads easily to abuse, even among those who have acquired it through their own extraordinary virtues. To see the working of miracles as an ambition or end in itself would be a denial of the aims of Buddhism, and indeed of most other religions.

Those who seek the ultimate wisdom of Hinduism have often found that everyday life and the demands of the body are a distraction to their main object. Enclosed religious orders are but one way in which a separation from worldly affairs has been used to enhance higher states of awareness.

Those concerned with the supernatural often distance themselves from mundane life and practice techniques to control and subjugate the body; the Hindu sadhus are famous for the success of this type of training. Also known as "fakirs," sadhus can be found in most parts of India; they live outside mainstream society, either as solitary recluses or as members of sects, and spend years perfecting control of their bodies and achieving the fullest development of their souls.

Ψ

Ψ

LEFT: Misri Das, a young sadhu training for his later initiation.

ABOVE: **Vasanta Giri, a sadhu who has kept his arm above his head for 12 years.**

The aim of sadhus is the purification of self through meditation and the observance of strict ritual practises. For some the intellect is itself seen as a barrier to spiritual insight, since it is cluttered with the preconceptions and falsehoods of the profane world. The reality lies beyond this, and the containment of physical things is a necessary condition for its discovery. Celibacy is essential, both in order to divert sexual energy into the search for truth, and to avoid the family ties and distractions which come in its wake. Food is kept to a minimum and taken only as fuel, not for pleasure. Some sadhus vow to live on fruit or milk alone. Similarly shelter must be just that, not a comfortable home, and many sadhus move about constantly. Some go completely naked, even in extremes of weather, while others wear loincloths or distinctive robes. Most have unkempt, matted hair which is cut only on the death of their guru or mentor, and consequently is usually waist length or longer. They cover themselves in ashes or dye.

Some sadhus achieve impressive levels of physical control, and seem to be able to over-ride natural laws within their own bodies. There are sadhus who have remained with one or both arms above their heads, day and night, for years; known as *ek-bahu babas*, these sadhus risk permanent injury, especially if they do not exercise enormous self-control during the lengthy process of bringing the limb down again. The *khareshwaris* are sadhus who have taken a vow to remain standing day and night; many are disciples of the renowned Mahant Bhagawan Das, who stood for 28 years. Control of involuntary body processes can be even more impressive. Regulation of breathing and pulse rates enables the body to enter a state of suspended animation which mimics death and can last days or even weeks. During this time the soul is able to leave and travel in search of enlightenment. Other reported sadhu achievements include levitation and translocation – appearing in two places at once. Of the 5 million sadhus, only a small minority reach the highest levels of saintliness which such skills indicate, but the majority achieve notable successes in their quest for enlightenment.

With their somewhat unusual appearance and air of detachment from the world, sadhus encounter the same suspicion that all those connected with supernatural power attract. Some are thought to be sorcerers or magicians, and children are often threatened with being "taken away by the sadhus" if they misbehave. Sadhus learn the techniques of meditation and become adept at using mantras – repeated sounds and phrases which can be manipulated to powerful effect – as a form of prayer, petition, or communication with the gods. Mantras are the key to spiritual energy, but they can sometimes be used as spells. They have been used to cure diseases, but can also cause them; some mantras are thought to be powerful enough to kill, and fear of this presumed power often provides protection for the wandering mystics.

Sathya Sai Baba, born in India in the late 1920s, is a well-known sadhu who has been heralded as a modern miracle worker. Far from leading a retiring life, he undertakes tours of India which attract crowds of thousands of devotees hoping to witness his miracles. He is considered to be more than a spiritually advanced ascetic. Originally claiming to be the reincarnation of the Indian saint Shirda Sa Baba, he has progressed to the stage that his followers claim he is the incarnation of the godhead Shiva himself.

His miracles include the production of "Zibhuti" magical ash with healing powers; the production of objects from nothing; and the ability to translocate and to disappear. Preaching self-discipline and charity, he points out that these powers are available to anyone who will follow the spiritual path, for all of us have the potential within ourselves. Performing these miraculous acts has undoubtedly contributed to his success, and to the growth of what is now a sizeable organization. The miracles corroborate his claim to divine status and keep drawing the crowds of fascinated spectators from both Eastern and Western cultures. Although Sai Baba is a model of spiritual virtue and has succeeded in bringing education and hospitals to the poor of his region, inevitably he has also attracted sceptics who suspect that his miracles are more to do with skilled conjuring than divine power. But despite these claims, the personal and religious integrity of Sai Baba, as well as his charitable successes, mean that he continues to be claimed as a true miracle-worker.

BELOW: Sathya Sai Baba, the contemporary miracle-working Hindu sadhu, who attracts crowds of thousands to his religious audiences.

Ψ

ABOVE: **St Paul was converted to Christianity through a revelatory experience, then went on to preach that all mortals are potential miracle-workers.**

SAINTS

Miracles are not altogether unexpected from religious leaders, but it is also possible that ordinary people may be capable of miraculous acts if they are virtuous enough. According to St Paul, any Christian could gain access to the power of the Holy Spirit. For believers, the gifts of healing, working miracles, and speaking in tongues were amongst the possibilities. What mattered was the use made of such gifts: "Though I have the gift of prophesy, and understand all mysteries, and all knowledge; and though I have faith, so I could move mountains, and have not charity, I am nothing." St Paul preached that the sacrifice of Jesus had given everyone a simpler route to God, a straightforward path to the power residing in Him. Paul's own radiant conversion on the road to Damascus had enabled him to work miracles himself while shaping the emerging Christian religion. His message is that the power is there for those virtuous enough to take it; and, since his epoch-making writings, many have responded.

Ordinary people who have taken up the power of religious faith in the Christian Church are known as saints. They began appearing very early in Christian history, and have emerged in their thousands ever since. The newly established Christian Church began to question whether all this miraculous activity was appropriate, and whether some of it actually ran counter to its interests. The difficulty lay in deciding who were true saints and who were agents of more sinister supernatural forces. The process of accepting candidates for canonization became much more stringent after the Middle Ages. The mere existence of inexplicable events, clairvoyance, levitation, or speaking in tongues was insufficient. The Church looked for evidence of virtue and piety in the life of the would-be saint and set up tough standards of proof that the saint, either before or after death, had caused a miracle to take place. Then the miraculous act itself had to promote goodness and faith. Healing and helping others were acceptable, as was anything which deepened faith in others. Apparently pointless phenomena, such as the recorded elongation of the body of Sister Veronica Laparelli while at prayer in the early 17th century, were by then unacceptable as evidence of saintliness.

Most religious people were themselves aware of the pitfalls of spiritual powers, and have even found them inconvenient; many have attempted to conceal and suppress them. Among them was St Teresa of Avila, a Carmelite nun born in Spain in 1515, who experienced various mystical ecstasies, including levitation. Witnesses saw her rise from the ground, usually trying desperately to hold on to something in order to anchor herself. But they were implored not to make her experiences known, as Teresa feared the implications of publicity. Her canonization was straightforward; not only were her miracles witnessed, but she promoted a huge expansion of her order and wrote treatises on prayer and spirituality which remain classics today.

Levitation seems to be one of the more inconvenient spiritual powers. St Joseph of Cupertino was one of the most prolific levitators of all time. Born near Brindisi in Italy, he was of less than average

BELOW: St Joseph of Cupertino was constantly levitating, to the inconvenience of both himself and the Franciscan order of which he was a member.

Ψ

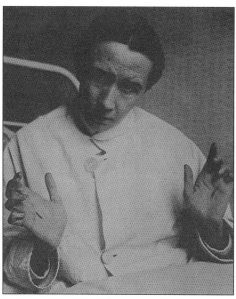

ABOVE: Some stigmata remain consistent over time but others, like those of Therese Neumann of Konnersreuth, Germany, appear or bleed only on religious festivals. The wounds on Therese's palms bled each Friday.

LEFT: St Francis of Assisi was already known as a deeply religious figure when he became the first known stigmatic, shortly before his death.

intelligence, but his piety and strong religious sense led to him being accepted by a Franciscan order in the early 16th century. It soon became apparent that any concentration of Joseph's thoughts upon religious matters could cause him to rise and travel some distance in the air. Numerous witnesses report him flying halfway down a church to arrive on the high altar, as well as through the open air into the branches of a tree. This happened so frequently that Joseph's levitations became an embarrassment to his order, who forbade him to appear in public and became very intolerant of him even inside the order. But there was no doubt of the existence of his gift, and no doubt either that he was a devout and virtuous monk, described as gentle and humble.

Sometimes spiritual power causes marked physical changes to take place in the body. The best-known case is the appearance of stigmata. These are bleeding wounds on the hands and feet, in much the same places as the crucifixion wounds of Christ. Some cases of stigmata have been fraudulent, but others have passed every test of authenticity. St Francis of Assisi was the first stigmatic. The five bleeding wounds appeared spontaneously after a period of prayer and contemplation, and remained with him for two years until his death. He refused to allow this development to be disclosed, for fear of attracting nonreligious speculation and interest.

Stigmata are associated with intense religious experiences. They begin with blood oozing through the skin and progress to actual wounds, sometimes passing right through the hand or foot. The wounds may remain bleeding and unhealed for months, or may heal and then reappear, often on religious festivals. Maria Domenica Lazzari, an Italian peasant girl, awoke one morning in 1834 with wounds on her hands, feet, and side; the wounds continued to bleed regularly on Fridays for many years. Having stigmata does not necessarily mean the possession of any other power such as healing, but it is generally accepted as proof of extreme piety.

One recent stigmatic is credited with other miracles, and has been put forward for canonization. Padre Pio (1887-1968) was an Italian peasant friar. A deeply spiritual man, he did not experience anything unusual until he began to develop pains in his hands, feet, and sides. Several years later, on the Festival of St Francis, he collapsed and started bleeding from these places. From then until his death 50 years later Padre Pio bled continuously from unhealed wounds and suffered unremitting pain. His devotion to spiritual matters increased as he ate and slept less and prayed more. His powers increased to encompass bilocation (appearing in two places at once) and healing. He is said to have healed a blind child and even to have revived a dead baby – miracles equal to any that the world has seen, and powerful and compelling evidence of spiritual power.

These miracles are under examination by the Catholic Church, which had been following Padre Pio's actions since the original appearance of the stigmata. Such controversial events are rare in recent times and the Vatican is generally extremely suspicious of people whose activities, if proved fraudulent, could reflect badly on the Church. Aware of this, Padre Pio attempted to conceal the onset of his stigmata and subsequently behaved with restraint; but there is no doubt that his effect upon his congregation was dramatic. Eye-witnesses describe the beauty of his spiritual ecstasy during Mass and the depth to which the devout were moved by his presence. If the Vatican is satisfied with the evidence and the canonization of Padre Pio proceeds,

LEFT: Padre Pio, currently being considered by the Vatican for canonization. He suffered greatly from his stigmata, and wore gloves to conceal them.

then the Church will have a major miracle-working saint for the 20th century.

Spiritual powers can also manifest themselves in visions, understood to be divine revelations. These can convey messages with concrete results. In 1858 a French miller's daughter named Bernadette Soubirous began to have visions of the Virgin Mary, although as an illiterate child she did not at first identify the subject of her visions. During one of them she was told that if she dug in a certain spot she would discover a spring with healing powers. Eye-witnesses watched her dig and saw water well up from the floor of a dry grotto. The place was Lourdes, and the grotto became the scene of nearly 70 scientifically unexplained cures, officially accepted by the Church as miracles. St Bernadette, as she later became, fell into religious ecstasy during her visions, all of which took place at the grotto. On her last visit her vision told Bernadette that she was not to return. Bernadette left in tears. Later she entered a religious order 300 miles (480 km) away, where she suffered various illnesses and remained out of contact with the world until her death at the age of 35. She never returned to Lourdes.

Today Lourdes is the leading centre for Roman Catholic pilgrimage. Over 4 million pilgrims visit the grotto each year, to see the shrine and collect some of the 27,000 gallons (123,000 litres) of water which the spring produces each day. Many of the pilgrims come in search of cures, and each day hundreds of sick and dying people visit the shrine in search of a miracle. Some receive a miracle, but most do not.

BELOW: Bernadette Soubirous, whose visions of the Virgin Mary led to the discovery of the spring of healing water at Lourdes.

Healing miracles are possibly the most fascinating of all. They confound doctors and scientists and provide a positive answer to the commonest question about miracles in general: whether they do, or have ever, really existed. The answer to this can never be entirely yes or no. Certainly there is doubtful authentication for many of the more impressive miracles, and modern illusionists are able to replicate many apparently miraculous feats without divine intervention. Yet it is true that events have occurred which defy explanation, events so powerful that they have altered perceptions and changed individual lives, and even the course of history. We are now coming to realize that the human mind is capable of more than was once assumed, and that our knowledge of natural laws is less comprehensive than we thought. The task of proving or disproving miracles becomes harder, not easier, as we discover more; St Augustine, as far back as the 5th century, wisely observed that miracles do not happen in contradiction to nature, only in contradiction to what we know of nature.

The central role of miracles is to direct attention

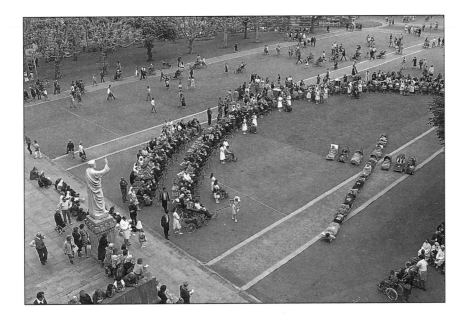

LEFT: Pilgrims form the shape of a cross as they patiently wait their turn to enter the grotto at Lourdes in France.

BELOW: The triumphant joy of one of the miracle cures of Lourdes: Marie-Thérèse Lepêtre, cured of Potts disease (tubercular deformity of the spine) in 1930.

to the power that may flow from goodness and love. Whatever the literal truth of the events concerned, miracles remind us that there is more to human life than science and rationality, that there is a spiritual side of our nature that continues to demand expression. As long as this remains true, pilgrims will journey to Lourdes in hope, and ordinary people will wonder if they, too, will one day encounter an angel.

CHAPTER III

MAKING THINGS HAPPEN

ABOVE: **The search for the Philosopher's Stone, the key to the perfectibility of all things, was the driving force behind the ancient art of alchemy. This 18th-century Rosicrucian document shows it as the goal of a metaphorical climb.**

I f human life is anything, it is uncertain. Each day we wake to new developments, many of them beyond our control or influence. Even the most ordered lives can be thrown into turmoil through sudden death or illness, accident, or alteration of circumstances. Minor events, though less dramatic, significantly affect the way in which a day proceeds. Although this makes life more interesting – think how much we look forward to the news, despite the fact that little of it is good – most people would prefer to have more control over the unknown.

Many belief systems, from smallscale preindustrial societies to major world religions, provide an explanation for the occurrence of both favourable and unfavourable events. Few beliefs are watertight enough to deal completely with unpredictable elements, and the ideas of scientific causality which underlie modern Western society, in particular, offer little except the concept of luck, coincidence, or chance. There is nothing to explain the random sets of circumstances which put an individual in the path of a drunken driver or in possession of a winning lottery ticket.

In a society which believes that chance is, by definition, beyond control, it is surprising how many people feel that small actions can affect their luck. If you doubt the prevalence of such deep-seated feelings, try finding a hotel room or plane seat numbered 13. Few people admit to being superstitious – the very word implies ignorance and a brand of prescientific thinking which should have been left behind – but this attenuated form of magic still permeates our lives.

ABOVE: **The frontispiece from a 1727 magic book. The spells and symbols changed little over the centuries.**

RIGHT: **A Serbian suitor follows an ancient superstition which holds that shaking the tree in a beloved's garden three times on a Friday will make her fall in love with him.**

SUPERSTITIONS

In this curious but very ancient segment of belief, magical methods are used to attempt a limited control over some of the whirling mass of fortune. Superstitions are part of folklore, usually disapproved of by the prevailing religious establishment and disparaged, at least publicly, by the elite. The basis of all superstitions is that the performance or omission of certain actions at certain times can induce either good luck or bad. Even the most rational members of our society know of many, and it takes a strong-minded person deliberately to ignore something which is said to bring bad luck. Superstitions may be positive – wearing a "lucky" item of clothing or performing everyday actions in a specific order – or prohibitive, such as avoiding walking under ladders or whistling in certain places. It may not work; but this rarely leads to the abandoning of the superstition. Failure can be explained by other factors, and the risk of giving it up is often too uncomfortable for the individual.

The basis for any particular superstition is often unclear, and usually complex. We can try to explain why spilling salt is bad luck by citing the times when salt was scarce and precious, but this cannot tell us why throwing yet more over our shoulder is going to cancel out the bad luck. To understand this we have to know, from the Middle Ages, that the Devil traditionally lurks at our left shoulder, waiting to seize upon the opportunity of some transgression such as spilling salt. We would also need to know that in medieval Europe salt was believed to ward off evil; throwing the salt in the face of the Devil would thus drive him off and forestall the bad luck waiting to descend.

Superstitions rarely yield to a single explanation. They are a combination of religious and magical beliefs, folklore and historical events, often long forgotten, which embody a cultural past. Exploring them leads us through a history of our forebears' symbolic thought. Although many of their meanings are lost to us, we retain our superstitions, possibly to focus attention on the more dangerous areas of life such as travel, illness, and childbirth. Superstitious rituals force people to attend to detail, and an "unlucky" incident can provide a scapegoat when things go wrong. A disastrous job interview can be accepted as almost inevitable if you managed to drop the mirror while getting ready. In the end, in situations where there is little more to be done, superstitions give us something, however tenuous, to do and to think.

It seems that the more unpredictable life is, the more prevalent superstitions will be. Farmers and other country dwellers are daily dependent on weather, seasonal variation, and the health of their animals; certainly their lives seem bound with the trappings of superstition. There is hardly any aspect of animal or plant behaviour which does not have an interpretation somewhere, and few tasks which have no superstitious beliefs attached. But those who left the land did not leave their superstitions behind them; in fact those parts of industrial life which are either crucial or dangerous are equally surrounded by rituals. Craftsmen had numerous prohibitions connected with their trades, and hazardous jobs such as mining were surrounded with prohibitions. There are still tailors who always sew the left side of a garment before the right, and building workers who ritualize their actions when working up ladders. British coalminers believed that it was bad luck to see a cat or dove near the pithead; that it was very unlucky for a miner to return home for a forgotten object or to see a woman on the way to the night shift. Anyone whistling underground would be accused of bringing bad luck into the pit. A survey of New England fishermen in the late 1960s discovered more than 30 recognized superstitions. The unluckiness of whistling and women turn up again, as does the prohibition on leaving port twice on the same day.

An investigation of superstitious belief among American baseball players in 1971 revealed that the more risky and uncertain the situation, the more superstitious activity there was. The players had a range of rituals, often personalized, to maintain their luck. These most often involved food and clothes, and commonly a player who had had a successful day would repeat his actions exactly the next time he played, eating the same food, wearing the same clothes, and doing everything in the same order. One player admitted to eating fried chicken at 4pm each day, closing his eyes during the national anthem, and changing shirts at the end of every fourth innings. In 1954 the New York Giants played 16 games without allowing their kit to be laundered in case their luck washed off. Sometimes the rituals become long and onerous, but as one player put it, "I'd be afraid to change anything. As long as I'm winning I do everything the same." At tense points in games players have rituals about tapping

BELOW: Cats have long had magical associations. Many superstitions surround them, the most common being that it is lucky to see a black cat coming toward you and unlucky to see one going away.

the plate with their bats, tugging their caps, or touching parts of their clothing between pitches.

Traditionally almost as superstitious is the acting profession. Careers hang constantly in the balance, and success is due to such intangible factors that prediction is almost impossible. Actors follow a long list of prohibitions: don't peep through the curtains, no knitting or knots near the stage, don't whistle, don't try for a perfect dress rehearsal, don't ever name *Macbeth* (call it "the Scottish play" instead), never wish anyone luck . . . and most actors add their personal superstitions and rituals to ward off disaster.

The power of a set of actions performed in a certain manner underlies all magical thinking. Not all repetitive actions are ritualistic; domestic tasks are performed regularly but only become rituals when their performance is thought to have more than face value. Millions of people empty their dishwashers at the same time each morning, but it is only a ritual if the emptier believes that his or her method can affect the outcome of the day. The power of ritual as a means of control plays a major part in the more aggressive and systematic forms of magic to which superstition is related.

BELOW: New England fishermen formed an extensive set of superstitions around their dangerous expeditions.

Ψ RIGHT: Sportsmen develop their own rituals and superstitions for important games. These are often most complex in professional sports where much can depend on the result.

THE ROLE OF MAGIC

The desire to take charge and control the power which determines our fate is one which requires more positive action and is usually linked to other ideas about the supernatural. Magic, from the Greek word meaning "great," can be employed to protect, to help, to enhance, and to destroy, depending upon the desires of the magician. It is this possibility of bending events to human will that makes magic so attractive. Unsurprisingly, throughout human history there has never been a society which has not made use of it.

Modern Western thinking regards magic as a primitive form of science, but the boundaries between science and magic are more blurred than they may appear. Much scientific belief is an act of faith on the part of most of the population; few of us have much understanding of the work of physicists, and much modern medicine works in ways which are not fully understood. Things that were believed 50 years ago seem ludicrous today, and similarly, we can assume that some of what we currently accept as fact will be disproved in the future. Belief, whether in something scientifically or magically based, is a powerful agent.

But over and above any practical effect it may have, magic plays a necessary symbolic and expressive role in human life. Possibly science and magic cannot be completely disentangled; many societies do not even try. Our conviction that there is a distinction between the natural and supernatural worlds leads us to try to analyze behaviour on this basis when it may not be fruitful to do so. An African farmer may not distinguish between careful preparation, watering and weeding of his crop, and the ritual he performs after planting. All are necessary for the success of his harvest.

Early travellers who brought back accounts of other societies found plenty of evidence of magical practices. They viewed these as a primitive form of science, part of a mistaken and ignorant theory of causality. Westerners of the 19th and early 20th centuries were caught up in the excitement of their new discovery – scientific thinking, which they opposed to superstition and considered a mark of their intellectual progress. They found marked differences between this and the

BELOW: Modern Westerners often confuse conjuring with magic. Illusions such as this levitating ball are for entertainment and have little to do with the role which true magic plays in a society.

Ψ

Ψ

60

Ψ

Ψ

LEFT: A dancer frightening away evil spirits during a harvest in Bhutan. He is using the power and drama of magic as a means of controling uncertainty.

dominant role played by magic in the small-scale societies they were busy discovering. Magic, to the Western eye, was the way that these unsophisticated folk attempted to influence events in the absence of higher knowledge. As time went on, more thought was given to the apparent differences in Western and non-Western ways of perceiving the world. Lèvy-Bruhl, a French anthropologist, wrote in *How Natives Think* (1926) that "the reality in which primitives move is itself mystical." "Mystical," for Lèvy-Bruhl, meant those forces and influences which, though not detectable to the senses, were still real and effective. As fast as Western society was rejecting magical beliefs in its own culture, it was discovering them in large numbers in those which it considered inferior. This made perfect sense at the time: it illustrated the chasm between primitive societies and those which were more highly

Ψ

Ψ

ABOVE: **This curse doll makes use of sympathetic magic. Harm done to the doll will be reflected in illness and pain in the living person.**

evolved. As anthropology grew and developed it became apparent that this simplistic view was of little value, but by then much had already been lost. Missionaries, traders and administrators had swept away the despised practises, consigning to history an enormous variety of magical and mystical thought.

Even as this process was taking place, however, Europeans witnessed events which gave them serious doubts about the "foolishness" of local beliefs. Some acknowledged that things were different in places saturated with supernatural belief, and that the scepticism of the Westerner was out of place. Missionaries in Africa during the late 19th century frequently saw extraordinary cures, watched objects moving violently without apparent cause, and witnessed feats of levitation. Subsequently anthropologists and administrators have given accounts of the apparently inexplicable events which make up everyday life in other societies, and we are better able to see the part which attitudes to the supernatural play in their lives.

BLACK AND WHITE MAGIC

There are common themes to magical thinking in different times and cultures. These were identified in the 1890s by Sir James Frazer, who in *The Golden Bough* made an exhaustive study of magic around the world. He realized that much magic relies on the sympathetic effects of similar shapes, colours, and properties, and on the feeling that things which were once in contact continue to act upon each other. Thus the ancient and widespread practise of making small images, dolls, or pictures of enemies illustrates the idea that damage done to the image will be reflected in harm to the real person. Spells upon individuals often involve clippings of their nails or hair, or items of their clothing – again pointing to the bond between objects and people. In Native American Navaho society a person's true name is very private and is not normally used, or, indeed, known to others. Possession of someone's true name would virtually guarantee the success of sorcery against them.

Individuals use the power they harness in various ways. The broadest distinction is between "white" and "black" magic. White magic is used by those who want to heal, to help, or to control fortune to their own advantage. Black magic sets out actively to harm or punish. There is a third category, counter-magic, which protects against the black magic of others.

White magicians set out to do positive things. In Europe, communities have had "wise" men and women since the Middle Ages. If you were ill, needed good luck in a particular venture, or felt under threat from some other supernatural agent, then the

LEFT: A 16th-century woodcut shows the magician Holler, who was reputedly able to travel across water.

wise woman was the person to see. The most popular requests were for love charms and spells to deter illness. Wise women earned only tiny amounts for their work, which mostly involved their considerable knowledge of herbalism. Often these skills were passed on from one generation to the next. Although wise people dealt in white magic, they were always regarded with slight suspicion. It was felt that the same skills could be used for less worthy purposes, and, unsurprisingly, when the witchcraze began (see Chapter V), the wise women were the natural suspects. Despite this natural tendency, many communities protected their practitioners, perhaps because they felt that their services were needed. When the witchcraze had burned itself out, many families of white magicians remained almost untouched by the upheaval.

Anyone who practiced magic found themselves with a double-edged sword. Even if their magic was protective and benign, they must inevitably hold the knowledge to perform more destructive acts. Suspicion could fall upon even the best intentioned, and one defence was to maintain as much anonymity as possible. Magical practise does tend to attract attention, however, and some of the more ambitious and active magicians decided to create a reputation which would ensure respect and a certain amount of fear. European sorcerers of the Middle Ages had special skills and magical tricks by which they were known, and their successes are described in medieval manuscripts. Holler, a famous Baltic sorcerer, was able to cross the sea on a small piece of wood without appearing to be in any danger of sinking. Sometimes the effort to make a reputation led to outright battles between sorcerers, such as that between Catillum, an Ostrogoth master magician, and his pupil Gilbert. Catillum was the eventual victor, and finally imprisoned Gilbert in a cave where he was held with shackles secured by a spell. Although he was eventually released by a third sorcerer, Gilbert's stay in the cavern made it a place of dread for the local population, who avoided it until the end of the 16th century.

Manuscripts also reveal some of the ancient spells themselves. Invisibility, an essential tool of the magician, was a commonplace skill. It could be achieved by various means, one of which was a device known as the Ring of Gyges. The ring was to be

RIGHT: Magicians have
always been suspected
of using their power
to do harm. Some
were thought to
conjure demons, as
this medieval
magician is doing,
to assist in their
black art.

RIGHT: Magicians have
always been suspected
of using their power
to do harm. Some
were thought to
conjure demons, as
this medieval
magician is doing,
to assist in their
black art.

made of fixed mercury, set with a stone from a lapwing's nest. Around the stone
should be engraved the words "Jesus passant + par le milieu d'eux + s'en allait". If the
ring was correctly made and in working order then it would not be visible in a mirror.
For the wearer to become invisible it was merely necessary to turn the stone inward.

More serious were love potions and death spells. Recipes for love potions in the
15th and 16th centuries consisted of such bizarre ingredients as doves' hearts, dried
blood and hares' kidneys, as well as assorted herbs. Difficulties arose with adminis-
tering the potions, most of which would have had a strongly unpleasant taste. Even
worse was the confusion that could follow when they were consumed by the wrong
people, as reported in the story of Tristan and Iseult, whose mistakenly conceived
love leads to their downfall. By the 18th century verbal spells and written signs and
symbols were preferred methods of directing affection.

Most death spells involved the familiar wax image or doll, into which needles
were driven and spells directed. Such spells were greatly dreaded by Western society
in the 16th and 17th centuries, especially by prominent people who felt that they
could protect themselves against physical attack, but were vulnerable to sorcerers.
Royalty were particularly concerned, and from time to time panics ran through the
courts of Europe. In 1560 Queen Elizabeth I of England summoned her astrologer,
John Dee, to protect her from a death spell after a wax image of her with a needle
through the heart had been discovered. Dee was a man with a deep and extensive
knowledge of magic; he had one of the most distinguished libraries in the country
and was known for his accurate astrological predictions and his flirtations with
alchemy. The Queen felt that he was the only person who could defuse the death
spell, and her faith was not misplaced. She did not die until 1603.

ALCHEMY

The Greeks distinguished firmly between low and high magic, and broadly speaking, this division is common to all cultures. Folk magic, though often used with good intent, has always been despised by those seeking higher knowledge and ultimate control. Despite its surprisingly high success rate it is perceived as base and utilitarian by those who are absorbed by the higher mysteries. Interest in high magic has ebbed and flowed through the centuries, but there has been a tendency for its adherents to become caught up with elaborate detail. The Cabala, the famous collection of mystical groups founded on Jewish scholarship, distinguished 72 names for the deity, 32 Ways of Wisdom, and 50 Doors of Knowledge. This tendency toward obscure language and over-elaborate ritual spread out into subcults and magical groups which emphasized secrecy and made much of their quest for the key to the mysteries of life. The fascination of these groups was considerable, and they flourished during the 18th century with the popularity of the Rosicrucian societies (harking back to the magical secrets of the Egyptians) and numerous minor occult brotherhoods. The combination of secret knowledge and the exclusivity of the powers it might confer was hard to resist, but the quest never seemed to yield anything more substantial than incomprehensible, though elegant, ritual structures.

The highest form of magic is the one which at first glance appears the most base: the search for a formula to create gold may seem to be more a case of greed than a yearning for ultimate truth. Alchemists have appeared through art and literature as demented early scientists, poring over roaring furnaces and bubbling retorts, trying fruitlessly to turn common metals into gold. In fact alchemy had very little to do

Ψ

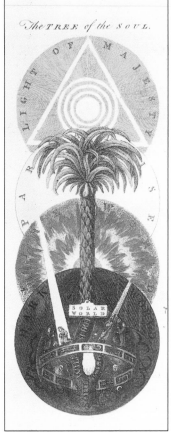

ABOVE: One of the enduring symbols of the Cabala, showing the worlds of Heaven and Earth connected by the tree of the soul.

LEFT: An alchemist at work. Many were so absorbed by the frenzied pursuit of their task that they lost interest in everyday life.

RIGHT: Alchemical illustrations were full of symbolic references, often reflected in strange images. This 16th-century print shows the importance of the three vital elements - salt, mercury, and sulphur.

RIGHT: Alchemical illustrations were full of symbolic references, often reflected in strange images. This 16th-century print shows the importance of the three vital elements - salt, mercury, and sulphur.

with primitive chemistry. The alchemical tradition was more about a quest for true knowledge and the search for perfectibility in human nature. There were moral, philosophical, and spiritual elements at work, as well as the physical manifestations in the laboratory. The alchemists were not content with elaborate spells – they were seeking to unlock the mysteries of the universe, and given that this was the true nature of their task it is not hard to see why alchemy has been one of the most enduring and engrossing of pursuits.

Alchemy is associated, above all else, with gold. Given its natural purity and low reactivity, which make it resistant to tarnish, corrosion, and fire, gold is the ultimate metaphor for beauty, purity, and endurance. It was thought to mature in the earth and to represent the highest state of matter, to which in time all elements would naturally develop. Gold had reached a level of perfection as yet denied to mankind and the rest of earth's constituents. It symbolized everything that the alchemists sought, and whatever could speed up the metamorphosis of other materials into gold was believed to have the power to do the same for the human body and the human spirit. The alchemical process can be seen as a compelling search for transcendency, in which the famous transmutation of base metals is merely a sideshow.

The extraordinary history of alchemy has lasted for more than 2,000 years in Eastern, Western, and Arabic countries. If it was nothing more than the apparently futile attempt to transform base metals, such widespread longevity would be surprising. This is not to say that alchemy has not had its share of materialists, many of whom were dishonest and fraudulent in their claims. But among its ranks have been the finest scholars of their time, many of whom considered alchemy the principal intellectual and spiritual challenge of their lives. The aim of alchemy was perfection: gold for metals and immortality and spiritual redemption for mankind.

Alchemy was recognized before the birth of Christ both in China and in eastern Europe, where Egyptian (even Cleopatra was rumoured to be an alchemist) and Greek traditions merged in a restless search for the key to the universe. The secrets of matter and the perfectibility of the physical and the spiritual were questions which raged through thinkers' brains. Although after some 500 years European enthusiasm waned while that of Arabic countries and the East continued to grow, by the 12th century Europe had rediscovered its interest in intellectual matters and alchemy was back. The Enlightenment rekindled developments in societies now broadened by studies in philosophy, science, medicine, and mysticism. Alchemy's emphasis was the wholeness of learning – its exponents were learned people who were familiar with most of the accumulated knowledge of the human race at that time, covering the fields of medicine, philosophy, astrology, mathematics, literature, and music. This depth and breadth, an impossible feat in today's world, made alchemy the most thoroughgoing attempt ever to synthesize a complete theory of human reality.

The first and most pressing task was the discovery of what was called the Philosopher's Stone. This was not necessarily a stone at all, but simply a substance which was capable of transforming baseness to perfection. In metals it could change common materials into gold, but in other areas it could confer the ultimate gift – complete knowledge and, with it, immortality. Such knowledge could banish the base elements of life as well as enable diseases to be cured, wars and disputes to be ended, and youth to be restored. The Philosopher's Stone, in short, was what everyone had always dreamed of – "the aim and end of all things under Heaven," the elixir of life itself. It was accepted that few could ever aspire to the ultimate achievement, and that most were doomed to failure. Whole lifetimes were dedicated to the quest, which was notable for the large numbers of those who wandered into error, deceit, and destitution along the way. The search took place partly in the laboratory and partly in the mind of the alchemist. Many of the mental techniques recall the actions of the shamans – seeking spiritual guidance through dreams and visions, and reaching toward a sight of a different truth through meditation.

Each culture, period and individual has brought its own approach to finding the answer, which may help to explain why no two accounts of alchemical processes are the same. But despite huge differences in cultural and religious backgrounds, alchemists everywhere have been doing recognizably the same thing. Broadly speaking three different strains emerge, each with its own emphasis. One concentrates on the physical world of metals and materials, the tangible world of laboratories and experiments. Another conceives of the Stone or Elixir as a curing, healing agent and works with herbs and chemicals in their medicinal sense. The third branch deals with the philosophical and mystical side of human nature, seeking to illuminate the deepest truths about our lives and our place in the universe.

Each branch of alchemy incorporates aspects of all the others, but puts the emphasis in a different place. The common themes are the identification of the "first matter," from which the Stone can be prepared, and the various methods of purification of the three vital ingredients, salt, mercury, and sulphur, each of which is heavily laden with symbolism. From the purified elements would eventually come a newly bonded whole, representative of the spiritual change which comes over the alchemist during the process – his transmutation to perfect knowledge and psychic strength. Here is one of the chief differences between alchemy and science: the scientist strives for objectivity, while the alchemist craves total personal involvement. The whole

ABOVE: The image of the Rosy Cross, derived from ancient Egyptian alchemical roots, was the symbol of the Rosicrucians.

point of alchemy is the identification between the process and the practitioner, and their simultaneous growth. This intense involvement goes some way to explaining the almost obsessive behaviour of alchemists.

Variation arises also from the personal nature of alchemical insight; one of the themes running through the centuries is the revealing of secrets through dreams, visions, and revelations. These are variously described as "gifts of God" or visits from guiding spirits. Alchemy has always been a solitary occupation, and not all its practitioners have had teachers to help them; many have had to rely solely on revelation and inspiration. Nicholas Flamel was leading the life of a perfectly ordinary 14th-century Parisian scribe when he dreamed that an angel was offering him a manuscript. When he awoke the manuscript had gone, but some years later Flamel recognized it among some others and brought it home. He realized that it was an alchemical text, but was unable to understand it. He began to read and research all he could, finally going to Spain to seek help. There the text was recognized as part of a lost book and partially interpreted. Flamel returned to Paris to continue his work, which he claimed was at last successful when he produced gold in 1382.

The alchemists themselves have come from every sector of society, ranging from the villain in search of quick profit to the poor devotee whose efforts totally bankrupted himself and his family. Committed alchemists spent every waking hour at their task and consumed huge quantities of equipment, fuel, and metals in the endless process of burning, and distilling. Many had rich sponsors whose interest was often merely mercenary. They often made hard taskmasters, however, as many of the II Holy Roman Emperor Rudolph's protégés discovered. Rudolph poured considerable resources into his 17th-century alchemists and their laboratories, but failure could be punished by torture and even death. Still, there seemed to be no shortage of applicants, and there was even a street in Prague, called Golden Lane, where his alchemists lived and laboured. Alchemy attracted the educated and the ambitious but their lives were never easy. In its true sense it is the path of dedication, and those best placed to pursue it have been those wealthy enough to devote time and money to the quest.

Somewhat surprisingly, alchemy has maintained an amicable relationship with the Christian Church during its 2,000 years of existence. There have been occasional outbreaks of repression, but these seemed directed mainly against dishonest metal workers rather than the true alchemists. Many early alchemists were monks, and numerous medieval churches bear alchemical symbols. Indeed, the Great Porch of the Cathedral of Notre Dame in Paris has been interpreted as a complete guide to the alchemical process, depicting all the familiar symbols and allegories of the art.

Most alchemists believed that at some time in the past the Secret had been revealed and the Stone made reality, and much of the quest revolved around finding hidden texts and coded revelations. So, despite periods of comparative openness, alchemy and its adherents have always been associated with mystery and secretiveness. Nothing about alchemy is plain or straightforward, and a typical alchemical document is virtually incomprehensible to the untutored eye. Layers of symbolism, metaphor, and allegory protect the knowledge and restrict its use to the initiated, and only a limited amount of information has ever been written down. Because of this deliberate obscurity, and the inevitable curiosity of the greedy, the art and its practitioners have usually been viewed with the suspicion and hostility that accompany all arcane pursuits. Alchemy has been banned at various points in history, beginning with the Roman Emperor Diocletian, who in the 3rd century burned all the available texts (mostly Egyptian) and forbade its practise. This paranoia has sometimes put alchemists themselves in danger, and they have responded by protecting their secrets even more carefully. Ramon Llull, a Catalan philosopher and a missionary who regarded alchemy as a sacred pursuit, cautioned his readers in the 13th century that "if you reveal this, you shall be damned," while later, in the 15th century, the English alchemist and philosopher, Thomas Norton's fears were for the unscrupulous use of such powerful knowledge. He wrote: "This art must ever secret be. The cause thereof is this, as ye may see: if one evil man had thereof all his will, all Christian peace he might easily spill."

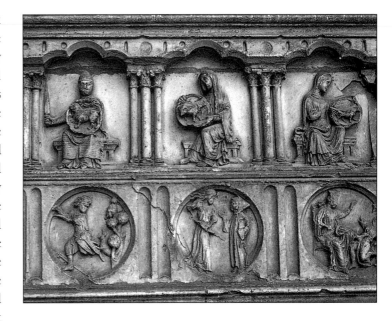

ABOVE: Alchemical references appeared everywhere in the Middle Ages, and were acceptable to the Church. These figures, with their alchemical symbols, can be found on the facade of the Cathedral of Notre Dame in Paris.

So concerned were alchemists with safeguarding the knowledge they had painstakingly acquired that elaborate hiding-places were devised for crucial documents, and dense codes were employed in their writings. The Arab alchemist Abu Musa Jabir, who was known as Geber, was skilled in music, art, and mathematics and in the 8th century invented a notation system which was reaching toward the modern system of chemical equations. So difficult and complex was this notation that it gave rise to the word "gibberish." The elaborate symbolism which surrounds alchemy is partly a function of secrecy, although the metaphorical nature of the quest delights in this form of expression. Both art and music are involved; alchemy has given rise to a series of beautiful and historic pictures which incorporate complex symbolism and can be almost infinitely interpreted. The iconography can be decoded to give quite precise accounts of alchemical processes. Baroque music has been held to be inspired directly by the deliberations of the alchemists. The music of the Italian composer Monteverdi (1567-1643), thought to have been an alchemist himself, appears to incorporate alchemical principles in its structure.

There was, however, yet another reason for secrecy. Much of the routine work of alchemy was considered a discipline to enhance spiritual awareness. The endlessly repeated tasks, the minutiae of the experiments, the withdrawal from the world which the process implied, were all part of the process of spiritual growth and refinement. The constraint of secrecy was an added self-denial, and the alchemist with his developing knowledge was compared to the sealed glass vessel in which the alchemical materials were heated as their transformation took place. Some alchemists never had the satisfaction of confiding their achievements to anyone, and most left only obscure accounts of their work.

It is intriguing to speculate whether any of the legions of alchemists ever succeeded in their quest. Serious practitioners could never reveal their breakthroughs in public but hints and rumours abounded. The proof of success, the achievement of the Philosopher's Stone, is instantly identified by the creation of gold. There have

Ψ RIGHT: Albertus
Magnus, shown at
work with his
manuscripts, was one
of the alchemists who
was reputed to have
succeeded in
discovering the
Philosopher's Stone.

Ψ

been stories and sudden *frissons* of excitement, but never anything unequivocal. In
the early 1600s a rumor swept Europe that a Count Moritz in Germany had cracked
the secret and produced gold to prove it. The alchemist network was alive with speculation and interest all over Europe redoubled, but nothing positive emerged.

This incident was typical of the sudden peaks of excitement which accompanied
the most intense period of alchemical activity. The most arresting story was probably
that told by Helvetius, a 17th-century court physician in The Hague in Holland.
Renowned for his love of rationality, he was a scrupulous and well-respected person
of great wisdom. Helvetius described a visit from a stranger who claimed to know
the Secret and who eventually agreed to give him a tiny sample of the Stone.
Helvetius duly followed his instructions and, to his amazement, produced from lead

LEFT: Thomas Aquinas, the most influential of the medieval theologians, believed that alchemical activities were dangerous; he was thought to have destroyed the successful formula of Albertus Magnus.

RIGHT: Nicholas
Flamel and his wife
Perrenelle. Flamel was
a dedicated 14th-
century alchemist who
was generally
acknowledged to have
produced gold and
used it to finance
charitable works.

RIGHT: Nicholas Flamel and his wife Perrenelle. Flamel was a dedicated 14th-century alchemist who was generally acknowledged to have produced gold and used it to finance charitable works.

a quantity of gold, attested to as pure by the town assayer. His amazement at this event, and his absolute certainty that it had taken place, made him a most credible witness, and his account still stands. Some commentators have interpreted his story as an allegory demonstrating his understanding of the true alchemical purpose, but it is not clear whether this was his intention.

Albertus Magnus, a Dominican monk who lived in the 13th century, was also rumoured to have discovered the Philosopher's Stone. He was a leading intellectual, interested in most subjects including alchemy, but sceptical about the possibility, or indeed desirability, of creating gold. Despite this it was persistently maintained that he had perfected an elixir which could cure illness and even bring a statue to life. His pupil Thomas Aquinas, who became an influential Catholic theologian, acknowledged alchemy but thought that it had diabolical origins. It was generally thought that Aquinas destroyed the Elixir after Albertus Magnus's death.

Later in the same century Nicholas Flamel, the French alchemist who had begun his journey towards knowledge after a revelatory experience, claimed success and appeared to prove it by his suddenly acquired wealth, which he used to build numerous hospitals, chapels, and churches. Although officially buried in 1418, there were reports of his continuing immortal existence as much as 300 years later and various alchemists in later centuries claimed to have met and talked with him.

Like many other essentially mystical pursuits, alchemy has never really vanished; modern cultures are once more taking an active interest in this most fundamental of questions. In 1919 the British physicist Lord Rutherford succeeded in transmuting nitrogen into oxygen. Although the process was a tortuous one, involving radioactive energy, its success confounded the rationalist claim that such changes in elements were impossible. Suddenly science has found itself doing what alchemists had predicted for centuries – physical transmutation, albeit at subatomic level. Now particle colliders enable physicists to produce gold whenever they feel like it, although such a process would never be economically feasible. Today physicists concentrate on the oldest of alchemical mysteries, the structure of matter, and talk of subatomic particles behaving in ways which would strike chords with the most ancient of alchemists. Meanwhile psychoanalysts such as Jung were rediscovering alchemy in their search to identify the deep workings of the subconscious mind, and alchemical material was inspiring research over wide areas.

While alchemical principles were inspiring research in new areas, the familiar arena of high magic continued to feed upon the secrets of alchemy. Rosicrucianism, a system of occult magic which developed during the 17th century, incorporated alchemical thinking, and this alchemical strand continued through to the occult groups of the present. The Hermetic Order of the Golden Dawn, formed in England at the end of the 19th century, came to be typical of these highly ritualistic magical groups whose members believed that it was possible to discover and use methods of controlling basic forces and, consequently, events. Its members included the Irish poet W. B. Yeats and Aleister Crowley, possibly the most famous British magician; all claimed success in discovering fundamental secrets and powers. Crowley claimed to have mastered invisibility, and even to have made himself immune to mosquito bites. He wrote at length about his methods and discoveries, and gave as his definition of "magick" (he liked to spell it with a "k") "the science and art of causing change to occur in accordance with will." Although the Hermetic Order of the Golden Dawn was short-lived – it collapsed from internal dissension during the early years of the 20th century – its influence was enormous, and groups derived from its teachings continue to dominate magical practise in Europe and North America to the present day. These modern occult groups operate secretly, much along the traditional lines of high magic, but they can be traced through the growing body of occult books and magazines which are available through specialist bookshops and centres. The considerable popularity of such publications shows that the attraction of magic has not waned.

BELOW: Aleister Crowley, whose interest in the occult helped shape the 20th-century high magic movements.

Do what thou wilt shall be the whole of the Law

CHAPTER IV

PLACATING THE GODS

ABOVE: A Bolivian
miner chews coca
leaves to dull the
effects of his hard and
dangerous life. Miners
offer regular sacrifices
to the mountain
spirits which are
thought to control
events underground.

High in the Bolivian Andes, tin miners beginning their week's work in the mines of Cerro Rico (the Hill of Wealth), pause in front of a demon-like effigy and make offerings of their most precious commodities – coca leaves, cigarettes, food, and alcohol. They are doing what people have done for centuries: identifying a controlling deity in their lives and making sacrifices to it. For the miners, Quechua and Aymara peoples who have worked here since the 16th century, this dialogue with the guardian figure of the mine is as essential to their work as their mining helmet and light.

In Bolivia, Catholicism was introduced 400 years ago by the Spanish imperialists, but the ancient Andean gods and spirits survive alongside the Christian beliefs, woven together into a flexible, syncretic religion. Traditional Bolivian beliefs recognized a god who inhabited the mountain, who first directed human attention toward the rich ore deposits and who is responsible for everything that happens in the mines. This god has taken on a Christian facade, similar in appearance to a devil; known as El Tio (the Uncle), he presides over life in the mines. His image must be placated with offerings and ritual, otherwise the rich veins of ore will not be revealed and accidents will occur.

The offerings are made weekly to maintain the dialogue. If an accident does occur, it is felt that El Tio, starved of food, has embraced the victims for his own sustenance. Then a complex three-day ritual is held in which llamas are sacrificed to feed El Tio and divert his attention from the miners. A good outcome (for example, the discovery of a new seam the day after the ceremony) would confirm the effectiveness of the ritual. An unfortunate one, such as another accident, would point to errors in the form of the ritual or to an unprecedented increase in El Tio's appetite which must be addressed with further offerings.

ABOVE: This ancient
illustration of
cauldron sacrifice
shows how some
Celtic ceremonies
required the giving up
of human lives.

RIGHT: Traditionally,
herdsmen such as this
North African will not
kill their animals
simply for food but
will sacrifice them
during religious
ceremonies, and then
eat them.

El Tio represents a powerful deity so strongly identified with the mountain and the mine that events within it are thought to be completely in his control. Humans working within this dangerous place must maintain good relations with El Tio if they are to avoid the misfortunes that so easily occur, and they do this in the way that good communications are established everywhere – by making gifts. Those who exchange presents have a relationship, different in kind from those who buy and sell, and the offering of gifts expresses the desire to initiate such a personal connection.

THE NEED TO CONTACT DEITIES

A glance at history reveals a strong urge for humans to communicate with the forces which control destiny. If these forces have been conceived as spirits or deities, there are sound reasons for wanting to contact them, please them, and incline their favour toward mere mortals. Sacrifice offers one solution; countless cultures have offered grain, animals, and occasionally humans as part of their relationship with their divinity. It may be that the gods rely upon humans for their very sustenance; some, such as El Tio, require constant feeding and make continual demands, while others are content with a share of the feast.

The incidence of sacrifice varies, and may become almost obsessive; the Ifugao people of northern Luzon, in the Philippines, make some kind of sacrifice almost daily. They are a prosperous agricultural group who combine traditional beliefs with certain elements of Christianity, and a democratic form of administration with an ancient system of kin-group feuding and revenge killings. An individual is at the mercy of the actions of other family members: he may be killed in revenge for a relative's behaviour, or required to carry out a killing himself in order to avenge the murder of one of his kin group. Anthropologists have speculated that the high levels of insecurity generated by this system contribute to the daily need of Ifugaons to placate the various supernatural beings which traditionally control individual destiny. There are deities responsible for almost every action that an Ifugao performs. However, these beings are not revered or worshipped, but are perceived as powers which must be appeased, almost bribed, to provide a successful outcome. The regular sacrifices of chickens, pigs, and buffalo are expensive, but necessary, insurance policies.

Whatever their forms, sacrifices are ways of opening up a channel to controlling forces, conduits for messages between the two worlds, and a means of approaching the very source of life. By its nature this is a dangerous task, and sacrifices are always surrounded by protective ritual; the careful performance of rites provides some safety to those who draw near to the unknown. Sometimes only ritual specialists are skilled enough to attempt such proximity, and laymen must make their approach through a priest or shaman.

Ritual also performs the vital role of alerting the deity to the sacrifice by addressing it to its intended recipient. It is difficult to be sure that a sacrificial gift has been accepted, because deities do not carry off the offerings. One solution is to burn the sacrifice, reducing it to its essence, which is carried up in smoke. Another view is that the offering is itself enough; the life of the animal or plant is the real sacrifice, and the remains can just as well be devoured by the participants as left to rot. In

LEFT: Brazilian Mehinacu villagers leave offerings for the spirits who influence the growth of crops.

Ψ

Ψ

societies such as the Nilotic cattle-herding Nuer of the southern Sudan, meat is only eaten after sacrifices. Cattle are too important to be killed just for food; but once their lives have been offered to the gods, the remaining carcass can be consumed.

The offering itself is often important precisely because it is a sacrifice – a gift of something valuable. Of all the possible offerings that can be made, the most power-ful one is blood – and the most compelling the blood of a loved one. Thus, in bibli-cal times Abraham was asked to sacrifice his beloved son Isaac to prove his commitment to God. The sacrifice was not in the end required of him; once he had demonstrated his willingness to perform it, his obedience was acknowledged with the restoring of his son. More capricious gods might require sacrifices merely to ensure their cooperation. In Greek mythology, Agamemnon, needing a favourable wind in order to go to war, was prepared to sacrifice his daughter Iphigenia to please the goddess Artemis – a fairly inadequate reason according to his wife, Clytemnestra.

HUMAN SACRIFICE

Considerably rarer than the more commonplace offerings of grain and animals, human sacrifice in the present day is restricted to remote tribal areas and, possibly, as part of occasional aberrant cult rituals. There are plenty of historical examples, however. Evidence exists, both from archeological findings and from contemporary Roman accounts, that human sacrifice occurred among the Celtic societies of western Europe and Britain from about the 3rd century BC to after the birth of Christ. Religion permeated Celtic life, and an essential aspect of it was sacrifice, including human sacrifice; so important was it that druid chiefs used exclusion from sacrifice ceremonies as an effective sanction against rebel individuals or groups. The druids were the priestly group within Celtic cultures; they were scholars, the guardians of traditional knowledge, from the nature of the supernatural and the structure of the cosmos to the law and its application. They were consulted on everything connected with these matters, and administered both religious and secular matters. The druids were famous for their divinatory skills, for mathematical divination as well as the interpretation of signs and portents in the natural world, and were considered by the Romans to be skilled philosophers and theologians and successful communicators with the gods.

Celtic human sacrifice took various forms, but all were directed towards propitiating the gods, whose identities and natures were described in the vast oral literature of which the druids were the guardians. The usual concerns, about harvests, health, and protection from foes, seemed to have been among their reasons for communicating with the deities. The victims were probably prisoners of war, criminals, and even volunteers. At least one of the sacrifice rituals, in which the victim was struck with a spear or dagger from behind and left to die, was linked to divination. The druids observed the death throes and made predictions based on their interpretations. Other victims were shot with bows and arrows, often in large numbers and possibly as part of the sanctification of temples; many were decapitated and dismembered. Surviving standing stones from druid temples contain niches into which human skulls are set, and an excavated shrine at Ribemont-sur-Ancre in France revealed the bodies of over 1,000 men and women, apparently ritually slaughtered and buried within the temple area. On occasions there was an extraordinary mass sacrifice; a huge, hollow, woven wicker figure was made, and into its colossal form were crammed living people. The whole thing was then set on fire, creating the powerful image of a burning human effigy in which dozens of lives were lost.

A cornerstone of druidic belief was that human souls were immortal. The afterlife, as illustrated in a carved stone sarcophagus from the period, was expected to be

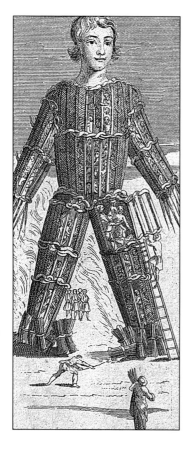

ABOVE: Classical observers were intrigued and appalled by the Celtic tradition of setting fire to a wicker figure crammed with sacrificial victims.

a continuation of the present one, or at least a projection of the main features of earthly existence. The dead were provided with objects and artifacts, or carvings of them, to equip them for the next stage. Given this belief, the practise of human sacrifice may not have been as shocking within their culture as it appears today. Even so, it met with the disapproval of the classical world, in which it was considered evidence of barbarism. From the 1st century AD, the Celts came under pressure from the occupying Romans to abandon their religious practises. Despite the distaste and

LEFT: A druid priest, portrayed by Roman witnesses. Rituals such as the sacrifice ceremonies were central to Celtic life, and exclusion from them was a major punishment.

Ψ

Ψ

ABOVE: The pre-Columbian Aztec empire was a successful and prosperous agricultural society. Tenochtitlan, shown here, was its capital.

scorn expressed by the Romans, they had only just abandoned human sacrifice themselves; as recently as 114 BC two Greeks and two Gauls had been sacrificed as an appeasement to the gods in Rome, and the practise had only been outlawed by Senate decree in 97 BC. But the increasing Romanization of western Europe demanded the dismantling of the indigenous religion, and the sacrifice rituals were an obvious first target; druids and their religion were gradually erased.

For those societies which practice sacrifice, the ceremonies are naturally regarded as an important part of both spiritual and social life. Sometimes, as with the druids, the ceremonies come to be regarded as so crucial that the very existence of the culture depends on their continuation. One society, the Aztecs, came to believe that only their sacrifices could prevent the end of the world.

When Spanish explorers found themselves on the coast of Mexico early in the 16th century they landed eagerly, in search of gold and other treasure. They found the gold, but they also found themselves witnessing scenes of pure horror – the ritual killing and dismembering of humans, offered for their approval. This was set in a culture of considerable sophistication: Technochtitlan, the capital city, was more than twice the size of any city in Europe at the time, and featured architecture on a scale which made the Europeans rub their eyes in disbelief. Gradually it became clear to the Spanish visitors that the sacrifices were considered essential by their hosts, who believed that without them the world would end.

LEFT: The sun, depicted here in stone, played a central role in Aztec belief. The Aztecs did not assume that this source of warmth and light would automatically appear – unless the gods were placated, it would die.

Their myths told the Aztecs that there had already been five worlds, five suns, and five circles of time. The first was consumed in a swarm of devouring jaguars, the second was destroyed in a great wind, the third by a fiery rain, and the fourth drowned in a deluge. After the fourth world there was nothing – just water, darkness, chaos. The gods Huitzilopochtli and Quetzalcoatl made the dry land. They dragged a monstrous female beast out of the depths, cut her body in two and made it lie on the water. From her hair they made the trees, from her skin they made the grass and flowers, from her eyes the wells and springs, and from her shoulders the mountains. But in the darkness the creature still cried out and refused to bring forth fruit.

ABOVE: A contemporary image of the moment of Aztec sacrifice.

Still there was no light, and no sun. The beautiful gods stood around a fire, wondering which one of them would sacrifice himself to make the sun. Finally Nanahuatl, who was small, sickly, and covered with sores offered himself and leaped into the flames. Then for the fifth time a sun rose in the skies, but unfortunately it took after Nanahuatl and was unsteady and weak. Quetzalcoatl realized that it would take the sacrifice of the other, strong gods to revive the sun and bring the fifth world to life. They made their sacrifice, the fifth world commenced and ever since then the Aztecs had been paying the gods back, offering human blood each day to ensure the continuing rising of the sun. The Aztecs were in no doubt that if they failed to do so the fifth sun would go out and the world would return to chaos. They felt that the gods required a heavy payment; each day at the various temples throughout the cities hundreds of living hearts were torn out of the sacrificial victims bodies and burned among incense in ritual braziers. Then the bodies were flayed, dismembered, and ritually distributed. Then the sacrificial sites were caked with blood and even the

Spanish arrivals, no strangers themselves to violence and death, were appalled at the scale of the human carnage and its seemingly incongruous role in a society so advanced in other respects.

The victims were normally either war conquests, carefully captured on the battle-field for this very purpose, or low-status enslaved groups, but there are accounts of volunteers willing to offer themselves in return for the privileged afterlife which was thought to await sacrificed individuals. Some ceremonies required higher status victims, whose deaths were surrounded by considerable ritual, while others relied on sheer numbers. The dedication of the temple of Huitzilopochtil, for instance, required the sacrifice of possibly 20,000 victims, their hearts torn from their living bodies at the top of the pyramid, their blood cascading down the sides. There seemed to have been a fairly cooperative spirit among the victims, who were generally not coerced along their final journey. It has been speculated that drugs were employed to smooth the proceedings, and undoubtedly in some of the more ritualistic ceremonies the victims actively participated in the events leading up to their inevitable deaths. Many of the victims had been captive for some time prior to their deaths, but they did not languish in dungeons; their care was given over to members of the local community, who fed and pampered them in their last weeks.

The Aztecs saw the universe as an insecure place ruled by the whims and appetites of capricious gods over whom they had little influence. An examination of

BELOW: Sacrifices were regular in Aztec society. Many of the victims were captured in battle, and it may be that the warmongering activities of the Aztecs were prompted by the insatiable demand for victims.

LEFT: A later depiction of Aztec priests extracting the heart of a living victim. The still-beating heart was the most effective sacrifice to gods who required constant gifts of the life-force.

Ψ

Ψ

their empire shows that to be a good description of their own society, which was rigidly hierarchical and constantly engaged in warfare, with subject nations and groups helpless in the grip of a ruling elite which they could neither comprehend nor influence. Resentment was rife in the outlying areas, and was barely contained by the military onslaught. The empire was overstretched and cracks were showing. The Spanish took advantage of this fragility to launch an attack on the empire and its riches. Assisted by the smallpox which they had brought with them, and amidst heavy slaughter, the conquistadores defeated the Aztecs and consigned their culture, their beliefs, and their sacrifices to history.

The Aztecs were not, however, the only people who practiced human sacrifice in South and Central America, although they may have been the most extravagant. New interpretations of ancient Mayan hieroglyphs and art show that offerings of human blood were an essential part of ritual life, and that the demand for victims was largely met by prisoners of war. The Andean civilization of the Incas incorporated human sacrifice into its rituals, although it was originally a more peaceful culture. Recently considered accounts by 16th- and 17th-century Spanish priests describe a system in which major sacrifices of animals, textiles, crops, art, and, finally, children were carried out in solstice celebrations which took place during tours of the Andean empire. The ceremonies were in order to please the gods, whose discontent was thought to threaten Inca fortunes. The children were specially selected; they had to be healthy, about nine or ten years old, and as close to perfection as possible – the ugly or deformed were barred. Selection was considered an honour, as the children were believed to become deities, according to the American anthropologist and South American specialist Johan Reinhard. They were sacrificed at key points of the kingdom, often on the peaks of high mountains, and contemporary accounts describe the victims being buried alive. Such sacrifices were believed to benefit the local community, as well as the general state of the empire.

The discovery of dozens of high-altitude shrines, some containing the remains of victims, confirms these accounts. A particularly impressive find was that of the well-preserved body of a young boy found in a marked grave on the 17,716ft (5,400m) Mount Plomo in Chile. The child, whose body had been preserved by the extreme cold of the altitude, is estimated to have died around the end of the 1400s, probably before the arrival of the Spanish in Chile. He was wearing Inca ceremonial dress, the details of which indicated that he did not come from the area in which he died, and was buried with gold and silver statues. He was found huddled, with his arms around his knees, his face peaceful and untraumatized. Later laboratory examination revealed no apparent cause of death but some signs of frostbite; there were indications that a nonlethal drug had been administered to him prior to death. The boy had been healthy, and his preserved features showed him to have been handsome. It was concluded that he had been placed alive in the grave and had died soon afterward from the effects of cold.

The custom of human sacrifice in South America was generally assumed to have died out with the destruction of the indigenous cultures brought about by contact with the Old World. But there is some evidence now that the beliefs of which the sacrifices were a part still persist, and investigations by the American journalist Patrick Tierney indicate that the practise itself is perpetuated in remote Andean areas, where its incidence is related to the threat of natural disasters such as drought and earthquake. Tierney uncovered evidence that men and women had recently been sacrificed to mountain deities by the Mapuche people of southern Chile, who were sufficiently determined and resourceful to resist both Inca and Spanish attempts at colonization. Even today, although administered by the Chilean government, they inhabit their remote homeland with little regard for the outside world. Despite the influence of Christianity, belief in the ancient gods of the Andes is strong; the Mapuche shamans still regard human sacrifice as the only kind powerful enough properly to influence the gods and mountaintops as the only suitable places to per-

RIGHT: Human sacrifice occured among Pre-Columbian Incas, but with far fewer victims than among the Aztecs.

form this ritual. It seems likely that a five-year-old boy was sacrificed in 1960, at the time of an earthquake and a tidal wave, and shamans admit that similar sacrifices have taken place since.

In addition, Tierney also discovered human sacrifices taking place near Lake Titicaca in Peru, where natural events are strongly linked in local tradition to mountain and earth deities. The sacrifice of a young man had occurred in response to floods in 1986, while other sacrifice ceremonies were known to have been conducted to "pay the earth." Tierney also found a sinister development in the area – shamans who could be paid to perform sacrifices for individual benefit. Businessmen, for example, appeared to be making sacrifices to improve their fortunes. In doing do they were following a very ancient idea that the gods could be placated and their power secured through sacrifice; success, in other words, can be bought with the blood of a human.

Human sacrifice has ceased in most parts of the world, but plant and animal sacrifice persists in many contemporary small-scale societies and has a continuing role in many Eastern religions. Chinese families in Taiwan and Hong Kong still keep family altars at which small offerings of food may be made to the spirits of the ancestors. Flowers are a common offering, and this is reflected in the Western custom of

ABOVE: **An altar in a Balinese temple, covered in flower offerings.**

85

leaving flowers on graves and, more recently, at the scenes of accidental or violent death. Offerings may be made regularly, or can be concentrated into fewer, more lavish sacrifices. The Gabadas, a small tribal people in Eastern highland India, hold sacrifices every few years to fulfil their obligations to the spirits of their dead. One buffalo must be sacrificed for each dead family member, and food provided for the guests, who may number over a hundred. A large sacrifice may cost a family more than a year's income. The sacrificial buffalo are closely identified with the deceased kinsmen, well cared for and decorated with flowers. After the sacrifice and feast, large stone slabs are added to the existing arrangement in the centre of the village; these represent the life-force of the deceased kinsmen, which is contained within the centre of the village for the benefit of the living community. The possible harm to be feared from the spirits of the dead is safely neutralized by the buffalo sacrifice. Animal sacrifices are reappearing in the Americas with the increasing popularity of voodoo and related belief systems. In mainstream modern western culture, however, sacrifice is the least represented of all the means of communicating with the supernatural. The Judeo-Christian tradition, in its later development, does not involve plant or animal sacrifice, but that in itself need not account for the absence of these ideas in the 20th century. But lacking a historical structure and expressive ritual to accompany it, the notion of sacrifice seems alien to Western thought and repugnant to current feelings about the role of animals in our lives. Placating the gods is still felt to be necessary, but other sorts of offerings, such as prayers, deeds, or ritual, seem more appropriate.

Ψ OPPOSITE: Pilgrims praying at Mecca. Members of Islam turn to face the direction of this most holy place whenever they pray.

Ψ

PRAYER

Prayer is a particular form of offering, consisting of words and thoughts directed toward a particular divinity or supernatural power; its targets can range from deities and saints to ancestral spirits or forces of nature, making prayer a near-universal part of human mystical behaviour. There is normally an accompanying ritual, such as a special place, body position, or pattern of movements, and the use of chanting, and incense or smoke, which symbolize the journey of the prayer towards its recipient. Effective prayer may demand fasting, sexual abstinence, curtailment of sleep, and other personal acts of self-denial, such as those practiced by those seeking the highest levels of spirtual development. But these refinements, although desirable, are not essential: prayer can be carried out anywhere, at any time, and can be either communal or solitary in nature.

The essence of parayer is communication, but there is also a sense in which prayers are offered as thanks and as worship, a gift of homage to the deity. They are acknowledgements of the divinity's right to humanity's time, effort, and attention. Having freely offered this, the mortal is then well positioned to make requests. Petitionary prayer – asking the superior power for help, protection or special gifts – is a frequent and widespread form, used for the benefit of both the group and the individual. There has often been disagreement about the appropriateness of personal desires as a subject for prayer. In medieval Europe the Church considered it permissible to ask God for help in virtually any circumstance; the English lawyer and states-

Ψ  Ψ

man Sir Thomas More, Chancellor to King Henry VIII, observed that criminals were turning to prayer for help in their crimes. Although more pious people felt that it was wrong to ask for a personal advantage that went against the good of others, most were happy to do so. In the Welsh border country of the 17th century, church records show instances of public cursing, in which aggrieved individuals called upon God to strike down their enemies; such action, though disapproved by the authorities, was none the less widespread. Modern Christianity recommends prayer as a means of communication with God, and allows petitioning for guidance and for gifts such as faith, as well as other benefits, both for oneself and for others; requests for material advantage, however, are discouraged.

Prayer may also be seen as a duty; in Islam the prayer ritual is elaborate and must be performed five times a day. The times of day, the attitudes, words, prostrations, and the ritual ablution preceding it are all included in the correct performance of the act of prayer. Its performace is an obligation; along with the profession of faith, the fasts, the legal tithes and the pilgrimage it forms one of the Five Pillars of the faith.

Much prayer is a balance between routine observances, communication, and petitioning. Prayer is widely considered a source of power and energy in itself. Going beyond rational thought, it can produce a higher state of awareness in which humans can cross the barriers between themselves and the divine. The 16th-century St Teresa of Avila described prayer as a progression, during which the individual gradually withdraws from the everyday world and concentrates entirely upon the divinity. Gradually, a state of quietness and calm allows the lines of communication to open until complete union and its accompanying inspiration can occur. In the major world religions the art of prayer has become highly developed and elaborated, but the state of mystical ecstasy which prayer can induce is experienced in some form in almost all known societies.

In closed religious orders prayer was the main focus of existence. Monks and nuns of many religions offer their prayers on behalf of the community outside their orders; they spend their lives working towards the religious experience which St Teresa describes and which is regarded as the most effective prayer state attainable.

There is evidence that prayer is an effective means of gaining the favour of the powers. Seventeenth century Puritans kept diaries in which they recorded spectacular prayer successes as part of their determination to show the effectiveness of their worship. Most individuals who pray on a regular basis can point to the effects of their efforts. Sceptics point out that failures are too easily explained: either the individual was not in a sufficiently pious condition when making the prayer, or the all-wise deity deemed it unsuitable, as part of a higher purpose, to grant the request. On an instrumental level, research in the 1950s, however, revealed an interesting result; a Los Angeles chemical engineer, the Reverend Franklin Loehr, established that trays of seedlings which had been the subject of prayers germinated more successfully and were more vigorous than equivalent trays which had not been treated in this way. These experiments have since been replicated by others, demonstrating that the psychic force brought to bear upon seeds and plants was linked to increased growth; these preliminary outcomes, along with positive results reported by the prayers of healers on plant growth, indicate an interesting area for new research.

Ψ

RIGHT: St Teresa of Avila was a mystic who regularly experienced divine revelations and wrote of prayer as the path to religious ecstasy.

Ψ

Individuals may find the effectiveness of prayer is linked to the opportunity it provides for calmness and concentration on a particular problem; often a solution presents itself during the contemplative suspension of worldly concerns. Many societies find communal prayers cement social ties and contribute to a sense of identity, especially in times of crisis. Even in today's Western societies, where churchgoing has declined, local disasters produce overflowing churches; acts of worship express the concern and solidarity of a community, as well as a sense of doing something positive in the face of overwhelming shock or grief. Even among the religiously unconvinced, prayer is a natural reaction to a sudden reminder of the powers which control our destiny – powers well worth placating.

HUNTING WITCHES

Every year, at the end of October, children in the United States, and increasingly in Europe too, dress up in costumes to celebrate what is variously known as Trick or Treat, Halloween, or All Hallows Eve. This ancient festival combines elements of both Christian and pagan traditions. All Hallows Eve is the night before All Saints and All Saints Days, when Christians remember those who have died and celebrate their lives; the date coincides with an ancient Celtic festival in which lights and fires were lit to drive off evil spirits emerging with the darkness of winter. The modern, somewhat commercialized version of Halloween embodies various stereotypes of the supernatural, and especially that of witches. In the ugly, wart-ridden old crone we see our cultural image of the witch – evil, threatening and strangely, smilingly triumphant.

For the majority of children, witches belong in stories and the annual rite of Halloween dressing-up. Some may know something of the time in Western history when witches were persecuted and killed. Most would be surprised to learn that witchcraft is far from dead and that there are more practicing witches today than at the height of the 16th- and 17th-century witchcraze (a useful term originated by the historian Hugh Trevor-Roper in 1967).

WITCHCRAFT IN MODERN WESTERN SOCIETY

Witches number over 50,000 in the United States, where witchcraft is a legally recognized religion, and there may be as many again in both Australia and Europe. When an American witchcraft organization, the Church and School of Wiccan, recently offered a correspondence course it was taken up by more than 40,000 people. Despite public reaction ranging

ABOVE: **Azande witchdoctors offer their communities an explanation for bad luck.**

RIGHT: **The fairy-story image of a witch – flying on her broomstick, complete with child, cat, and dog as passengers.**

from mirth to hatred, these witches are self-acknowledged practitioners of a belief system which they consider offers insight and practical help to members of modern Western society. Judging from the success of witchcraft books, journals, and magazines, they could be right.

The phenomenon of large numbers of educated Westerners, brought up in the scientific-rationalist tradition, embracing magic, ritual, and the worship of pagan gods causes a certain amount of controversy. In 1990 the composer James Macmillan wrote a musical piece entitled *The Confession of Isabel Gowdie*. Successfully performed in London, the music declared support for all those who had been victimized in witch hunts of various kinds, and it produced an unexpectedly large postbag. The reaction, both pro- and anti-witch, was notable for its depth of feeling and the deeply entrenched views of the correspondents. Witches still clearly provoke controversy, fear and hatred, but modern witches present themselves in an entirely positive light. Much of the negative reaction which they provoke can be traced to confusion surrounding the term itself. The word "witch" is so emotive and hung with cultural imagery that it is hard to divorce it from its stereotypes. This is recognized by some modern groups who call themselves "Wiccans" or "Neo-Pagans" and refer to "the Craft" instead of "witchcraft".

New witches practice a tradition which they trace back far beyond the unfortunate victims of the witchcraze hysteria to the ancient, nature-based religions of paganism. They look to the Druidic and Celtic cults which predated Christianity for a way to channel the spiritual power which they believe to be latent in us all. It is difficult to generalize too much about modern witchcraft; there are so many versions, each with its own variants of belief and practise. There are small and large groups, those who practice in covens and those who are solitary. Some are entirely secretive, while others openly proselytize for their belief. What almost all share is a rejection of the Judeo-Christian movement, a veneration of nature and the pagan tradition, and the channeling of universal forces to magical effect. Many differ in the elements of paganism which they have adopted, selecting and combining deities and myths in order to forge a new religion. Despite claims to the contrary, this form of witchcraft truly is a new breed, a modern belief system synthesized from traditional folklore and fragments of ancient motifs. There is no evidence for the romantic notion that witchcraft represents an unbroken line surviving, against all the odds, from its pagan roots, even though some of the ideas are indeed ancient.

In addition to the older traditions, some of today's witches believe in reincarnation of a straightforward kind in which the dead simply return, after a period of revitalization, to be born again as someone else. Many claim that this brings a new dimension to their lives, adding to their sense of continuity with the past. All witches regard the magical element as essential. Again we find a combination of styles, with simple magic of folk provenance, such as herbal potions, sympathetic magic (in which power is held to reside in association, so that spells may use hair or nail clippings of the subject), and divination, mixed with traces of high, ceremonial magic and astrology. Wax images go hand in hand with cabbalistic signs (derived from the ancient Jewish belief in the mystical power of the contemplation of letters and images), and the divinatory cards of the Tarot. The recurrent theme is of freedom and joy. Witches speak of fulfillment, security, and the release of creative energies.

Ψ

Ψ

LEFT: Members of a
modern druid order.
Many modern witches
trace their roots to
Celtic and Saxon
traditions.

Doreen Valiente is one of the leading figures in British witchcraft; working with Gerald Gardner, one of the most famous modern occultists, during the formative years of the witchcraft revival, she wrote many of the rituals and ceremonies in current use. In a recent film interview she describes the essence of modern witchcraft: "We believe in the hidden powers of the mind. We've got the paraphernalia and ritual tools that witches use, but what they really do is provide atmosphere, the aura in which those hidden parts of the mind, which I think everyone's got, can start to work and operate . . . it is a natural power, not an unnatural one, and everyone has it." She describes the link with paganism thus:

Witches have always believed in a Goddess as well as a God. They believe in the basic life force of the universe which they personify as the Old Horned God and the Moon Goddess. These are the earliest representations of a deity. We find them back in the painted caves of the Stone Age. These are the two sides of nature – if you like, the masculine and the feminine. We talk about fertility a lot, but today witches more often mean the fertility of mind – creativity, spirituality. I think more emphasis on this will be brought out as the Aquarian Age comes in. We hear a lot about the New Age. Well, witchcraft is going to be a part of it, very much so.

Modern witches feel that their religion gives them freedom, confidence, and spiritual fulfillment. But does it have other uses? Rituals are performed for healing, protection, and the influencing of everyday events, and witches are quite confident that they work. As Doreen Valiente explained to the film crew, "Today I asked very fervently for the power to provide you with a parking space for your van, and lo and behold, it did. Which is something contrary to the order of the universe, with parking the way it is today!"

The possibility of using such effective power in any but a benign sense is strongly denied. Today's witches claim to be non-aggressive, concerned only with developing spiritual potential. They do, however, feel a sense of identity with those earlier witches, and the link is clearly felt. As Doreen Valiente says, "Hanging us and burning us was a waste of time. We've come back."

WHAT IS WITCHCRAFT?

Witches are a recurrent theme across the world, never quite the same but always, somehow, recognizable. All societies are aware that some individuals appear to have the power to heal and to harm by magical means. Sometimes the two categories are separated, with different people associated with each role, but more often they are thought to go together, on the principle that if magic can be invoked to do good, then it can just as easily be turned to harmful ends. Whether we can discover a common thread and identify a universal witch depends on how we choose our definition. The word is used in so many cultures and contexts that comparisons can be misleading. It is probably most useful to start by defining witchcraft as the power to help or harm by supernatural means. Using this, we can find witches everywhere, but their differences are almost as marked as their similarities.

In non-Western societies witches tend to fit into the integrated belief system typical of smaller-scale groups; for many, witchcraft forms part of a general explanatory system in which the concepts of luck, coincidence, and fate are replaced by the effects of the ill-will of others. Witchcraft means that unfortunate events are not a matter of chance; you are ill or unfortunate because someone has caused you to be so by supernatural means. In some African societies there is even no such thing as an accident – you would not be in the wrong place at the wrong time if someone's witchcraft had not put you there. This is not to say that the witch has necessarily plotted your misfortune; the Azande witches of the Sudan and Zaire, for example, are born, not made. They act unconsciously, unaware that their resentments may be psychically influencing events. No spells or incantations are involved, and their witches are not considered culpable in the same way as, say, a murderer.

Those tempted to dismiss these ideas as fantastic should note that Azande witch-craft beliefs are perfectly compatible with scientific explanations. An Azande accepts that illness results from germs – but why did the germs make you ill and not your brother? And why at that particular time? Modern doctors cannot explain why two children in a house may get chickenpox, but not the third, who then goes on to catch it a year later. This is no mystery to an Azande – clearly a witch had aggressive feelings about only two of the children at that time.

The details of witchcraft in non-Western cultures may vary, but its relevance to other aspects of social life is fairly consistent. Witches in the European tradition, however, usually have a marginal position among the host of competing traditions. They do not fit so neatly into the scheme of things, and there is even uncertainty about whether a witch is necessarily bad. Non-Western societies view witches as unequivocally bad; early references, from the story of the Witch of Endor in the Old Testament (Samuel 1) and the condemnation in Leviticus 20, through the Greco-Roman period, where we find the rapacious, child-slaying Lilitu and Horace's repulsive Canidia and Sagana, are unanimous in declaring witches to be malevolent. In later Europe, however, the picture is less clear-cut. In medieval times, most villagers in Europe knew of a person who could do certain things. Called variously "witches", "wise men," "wise women" and "charmers" in England, and "hexenbanner" in Germany, these essential individuals cured illnesses, located lost objects, and made predictions to help the undecided. Writing of local wise people in London in 1638, T. Heywood describes " . . one Hatfield in Pepper Alley, he doth pretty well for a thing that's lost. There's another in Coleharbour that's skilled for the planets … Mother Phillips, of the Bankside, for the weakness of the back … and all do well according to their talent." The healers used a range of methods: Joan Mores, a wise women of Kent described in 1525 how she was able to divine the future from listening to the croaking of frogs. These were solitary practitioners, not members of a cult, and there is no evidence that they ever formed groups or covens. Their brand of healing combined commonsense remedies with a knowledge of herbalism passed from parent to child, but an element of magic was vital. Spells, charms, and rituals were part of the prescription. The roots of this magic lay in ancient pagan magi-cal lore, a mixture of Celtic and Norse traditions which emphasized closeness to nature and its

BELOW: A wise woman, using her herbal skills to heal a patient.

ABOVE: **This picture plays upon the typically ambivalent attitude towards the wise woman model of a witch – a solitary yet powerful outcast, regarded with both fear and fascination.**

secrets; the influence of Christianity, however, was unmistakable.

The charms used by medieval witches incorporated prayers and invocations of the Church, in both Latin and Hebrew, as well as more unconventional elements. Use was made of the mystic power of language, magical incantations being combined with texts already imbued with the potency of the Church. In England, an early 16th-century prescription for ague included wrapping the magic incantations "Arataly, Rataly, Ataly, Taly, Aly, Ly" around the patient's arm and then saying three Paternosters (the Lord's Prayer in Latin) each day. The combination of reasonably sophisticated herbalism and the enactment of a ritual clearly worked, and most members of the community took advantage of the skills that were offered.

These practitioners, both men and women, were known by the name "witch," but they had little in common with witches outside Europe, or with European witches as they were perceived in the following centuries. They were essentially working magicians, although they were paid only small amounts. The local population viewed them as positive, indeed indispensable, but there was always the suspicion that they could turn their skills in more dangerous directions. Popular wisdom tended to endorse the view that all magic has a dark side, and people inevitably wondered about the powers of the "wise" men and women. Some were known to put on curses for money, and love charms nearly always involved third parties who would suffer from them. If a curse was suspected, the sensible remedy was to visit a witch and pay to have the curse lifted, thus pitting the skills of one practitioner against another. When James Hopkinne of Essex, England feared in 1576 that his cattle had fallen under a curse, he went straight to Mother Pershore, the local wise woman, for help, confident that she could identify the curser and counteract the curse. And if misfortunes mounted up, where else would the finger point but to one who was known to have power over such things? As a traditional saying goes, "the witch who can't curse can't cure."

IN LEAGUE WITH THE DEVIL

Sorcery and magic were a universally accepted part of medieval life, and religion was regarded as a part of this broad canvas. The Christian Church embraced supernatural power in the form of its God, and miracles and prophesies were acceptable, even essential, evidence of a divine power. Developing amid a climate of magic, the Church had always gone to great lengths to distance itself from simple spells and stress its divine origins. Early Christians vehemently defended Christ from the suggestion that he was a common sorcerer. After the insulting claim by the Pagan Celsius that Christ was nothing more than a magician, Christians took to condemning sorcery in others (Elymas and Simon in the book of Acts) as well as underlining their leader's divine origins. By the Middle Ages Christ was firmly established as a divine figure, but magic and miracles were still readily accepted in religious life. There was increasing unease in the Church at the ubiquity of apparently supernatural events; the miraculous power of relics, holy words, and objects within the Church was beginning to be reconsidered by the clergy as their opposition to folk magic increased.

ABOVE: One of the everyday temptations of the Devil which so alarmed theologians in the 1500s.

All sections of the Church were concerned about the spread of superstition, by which they meant those magical ceremonies and beliefs unconnected with religion. They feared the adulteration of their teaching and the ultimate loss of their power. In 1484 the Catholic Church issued a Papal Bull which declared that no one but its own members was in contact with divine powers. The only miracles were those sanctioned by God and His Church, and anyone else making use of the supernatural must be doing so through the direct intervention of Satan. The Bull castigates such sinners: ". . . at the instigation of the Enemy of the human race they do not shrink from committing and perpetrating the foulest excesses to the peril of their souls, whereby they offend the Divine Majesty." God and Satan were opposed and there could be no grey area, no neutral or mechanical magic. By staking this claim the Church was declaring a whole area of supernatural activity to be illicit and, necessarily, evil. It was also committing itself to fighting these forces and those who made use of them. If witches had powers, they could only be coming from the Devil, which made them not only opposed to the Church but actively in league with the Church's (and God's) arch-enemy. Gradually attention focused on this belief, and Europe eased into an era in which tens of thousands of entirely innocent people were to die.

The new role of the Devil as the active opponent of God became more entrenched as the threat from this outside enemy engendered a sense of identity and purpose in a

RIGHT: Women, particularly, were thought likely to succumb to the temptations of the Devil and submit to his power.

Church weakened by dissent. The authority of the Roman Catholic church began to be questioned all over Europe, and the suppression of heresy, as this independence of thought was known, gradually occupied more of the Church's attention. Such a threat to the sanctity of the Church's doctrine could, it was construed, only be coming from the Devil, who was working towards the overthrow of the Catholic Church. Catholic scholars devoted themselves to further elaboration of the diabolic theme, issuing detailed edicts at regular intervals during the 15th century. The treatise *Cabinet du Roy de France*, published anonymously in France in 1581, concluded that there were more than 7 million demons, highly organized and working under the direct control of the Devil. As the medieval period drew to a close, Satan himself became an increasingly tangible figure, his horns, tail and cloven hoofs depicted in such paintings as the Limbourg brothers' *Tres Riches Heures du duc de Berry* (1415) and Fra Angelico's *The Last Judgement* (1430), typifying an image which persists into this century. The anonymous illustrators of *Der Ritter vom Turn*, a cautionary tract published in Augsberg, Germany in 1498, show how the Devil could be expected to appear with his temptations at any time in everyday life. And Satan could easily take other forms when it suited him, to tempt and mislead the unwary, although often one feature, such as the tail, would betray his identity. The development of printing meant that information and images handed down from the Church intellectuals could be distributed to the mass of the people. Although most could not read, the power of pictures brought the message, echoing the carvings embellishing churches and cathedrals such as Bamberg Cathedral, in Bavaria, and the abbey of Conques in Aveyron. The actions of the Devil and his earthly accomplices were known far and wide, and people became confident that they could recognize them.

Concern among theologians began to focus on the inner life of thoughts, dreams, and fantasies, the area of the soul now thought most vulnerable to attack. The Calvinist James Calfhill wrote in England in 1646 of demons which "appear to men in divers shapes, disquiet them when they are awake and trouble them in their sleep." A contemporary sermon speaks of evil spirits filling the very air – "I am not able to tell how many thousand be here amongst us." The Devil's threat was so great that not even the spiritually pure could be sure of protection. Prayer was essential, but even this was not guaranteed. One prayer, by the Englishman Thomas Becon, asks despairingly for protection against the "infinite number of wicked angels … seeking my destruction."

It is difficult for us now to appreciate the extent to which life in the 16th and 17th centuries became dominated by the struggle between God and the Devil, Heaven and Hell. Although the existence of the Devil is still acknowledged by religious leaders today, and some occult groups claim familiarity with Satan, the Devil is no longer perceived as a real part of our everyday lives. But 400 years ago the Devil was as real to many Europeans as their next-door neighbour. During the Witchcraze which followed, many of them came to believe that their neighbour actually was the Devil – or at least the Devil's disciple.

Everyone knew that Hell was waiting for those who succumbed to the Devil's temptations, but in the meantime he offered power. Many thought themselves equal to the challenge but feared that others in their community would be too weak to resist. Detecting the Devil and all his works became an obsession and the witchcraze grew directly out of the conviction that the Devil was at work and must be found and driven out.

Before the 16th century witches could be tried and punished for causing harm, but although they were thought to have used magic they were treated in much the same way as a thief or any other criminal. However as the Church began to draw a clearer picture of the Devil as a physical presence witchcraft practises became inextricably linked with the idea of a "Pact with the Devil," whereby witches succumbed to the Devil's temptations and agreed to carry out his work. It was this alleged alliance with the Devil which became the crucial feature of witchcraft trials and confessions.

HYSTERIA AND PERSECUTION

The ecclesiastical courts of Europe embarked upon the elimination of witches with the same zeal with which they had previously addressed the heretics who had questioned the beliefs of the Church. Torture was routine and execution was by burning. In England witchcraft remained a secular offence, tried in the criminal courts; torture was not condoned and death was by hanging. This meant a lower conviction rate than in the rest of Europe, but it should not be thought that England was less concerned with the antics of the Devil.

The King himself took a personal interest in the subject and lent his weight to the campaign to eliminate the Devil's agents. When in 1590 King James VI of Scotland (later James I of England, 1603 – 1625) was told about a conspiracy, led by his cousin the Earl of Bothwell, to kill him through witchcraft and sorcery, he was already a firm believer in the diabolical. James has been characterized as intelligent, open-minded, and very conscientious. He was aware of his duty as both a secular and religious leader. It might seem surprising that such a man was prepared, at least initially, to believe in broomsticks and spells, but the theological discussions of the time were extremely persuasive. James had spent six months in Denmark, talking with the theologians who were in the thick of the most urgent discussions about the

ABOVE: A contemporary illustration shows the main characters in the North Berwick witch trials, flying around a local church.

Satanic crusade. He had enlisted in the struggle, and identified himself strongly with God and the Church; it would seem only natural for the Devil to plot against him. He determined to discover the truth of the accusations against Bothwell, and arranged a trial of the witches allegedly involved in the treasonous plot.

Known as the North Berwick trial after the place where the alleged sabbats, or witches' meetings, occurred, these detailed proceedings, with their lurid revelations and eventual convictions, only confirmed the King's belief in the Church's warnings. Scotland, unlike England, permitted torture during the interrogation of witches. The North Berwick trial was faithfully recorded by a local church minister, James Carmichael. Although in no doubt himself about the guilt of the four accused, he expressed surprise that Agnes Sampson, the leading witch, who confessed only after severe torture, was "a woman not of the base and ignorant sort of witches, but matron-like, grave and settled in her answers, which were all to some purpose." After being questioned by the King in person in the Great Hall at Holyrood House, Agnes confessed to all sorts of extraordinary activities and behavior, many of which have become part of the stereotypical fantasy surrounding witches ever since.

Agnes confessed to having attended a sabbat with 200 witches on All Hallows Eve, and to going to sea in a riddle or sieve. She admitted performing rituals in the church at night where "the Devil himself started up in the pulpit like a meikle black man, and calling the roll, everyone answered – here! Then the Devil enjoined them all to a penance, which was that they should kiss his buttocks, in sign of duty to him." She confessed, recorded Carmichael, that they "took a cat and christened it,

DAEMONOLO-
GIE, IN FORME
of a Dialogue,
Diuided into three Bookes.

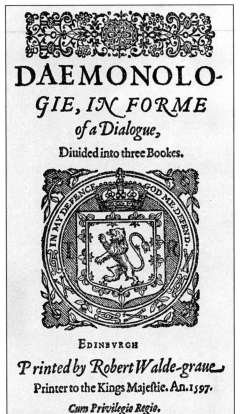

EDINBVRGH
Printed by Robert Walde-graue
Printer to the Kings Majeftie. An. 1597.
Cum Privilegio Regio.

ABOVE: A broadsheet illustration, showing Agnes Sampson on friendly terms with the Devil.

RIGHT: The title sheet of James I's book on witchcraft and the Devil.

and afterward bound to each part of that cat, the chiefest part of a dead man, and several joints of his body. And in the night following, the said cat was conveyed into the middle of the sea." This action was performed as part of a plan to create a storm, intended to shipwreck King James when he sailed from Denmark to Scotland. When it failed, the witches confessed that they tried again by delivering to the Devil a waxen image of the King. The reason that this also failed, confessed the hapless Agnes, was because the King was a man of God and so could resist the wiles of the Devil. Her final plan included the smearing of toad venom on clothing worn by the King, but that also failed. With these confessions, the witches were found guilty and burned at the stake on Castle Hill, Edinburgh. The supposed instigator of the plot, the Earl of Bothwell, escaped and fled to Sicily.

James's belief in diabolical practises not only gave political credence to the era of witch-hunting that followed, but influenced the whole climate of thought. Becoming immersed in the subject, in 1597 he even wrote his own guidebook to the menace, entitled *Demonology*. He included such statements as "assaults of Satan are most certainly practised and the instruments thereof merit most severely to be punished." His beliefs affected his most enduring monument, the translation of the Bible which, known as the King James Bible, remained in use for more than 300 years, and indeed is still the preferred version for many Christians. In Exodus 22:18 in this translation we can read: "Thou shalt not suffer a witch to live" – divine authorization for the prosecution and execution of witches. This sentence was to have profound implications, yet the translation is an inaccurate and misleading one. The original

ABOVE: The accused North Berwick witches, called before James I.

ABOVE RIGHT: The three witches from *Macbeth*, reinforcing an image of witchcraft based on James I's ideas.

Hebrew word in this sentence is *kaskagh*, which means "poisoner" or "sorcerer" in this context. It had previously been translated into Latin as *maleficos*, which at the time meant a person who causes harm – virtually any sort of criminal. To render it as "witch" changed its meaning and gave new support for the witch-hunters. It is unclear whether James was directly responsible for the sentence or whether the translators, knowing his beliefs, sought his favour by cooperating with them.

In other areas we can see how writers and artists, by seeking to flatter the King and pander to his interests, in turn influenced public opinion. Even William Shakespeare was not above this; the images of witchcraft wrung from such tragic figures as Agnes Sampson were perpetuated in *Macbeth* (albeit mixed with Greco-Roman elements such as the "Hubble bubble, toil and trouble" spell). Shakespeare drew directly on the evidence of the North Berwick and similar trials when he wrote the play, a few years after the burning of Agnes and her fellow witches. The first performance was given at Hampton Court Palace in the presence of the King and his brother-in-law, King Christian IV of Denmark. In the play, the witches and their activities parallel what Agnes Sampson and her fellows are reported to have plotted against King James:

> First Witch: But in a sieve I'll thither sail,
>   And, like a rat without a tail,
>   I'll do, I'll do, and I'll do.
> Second Witch: I'll give thee a wind.
> First Witch: Thou art kind.
> Third Witch : And I another.
> First Witch: I myself have all the other;
>   And the very ports they blow,
>   All the quarters that they know
>   I' the shipman's card.
>   I will drain him dry as hay:

Sleep shall neither night nor day
Hang upon his pent-house lid;
He shall live a man forbid;
Weary seven nights nine times nine
Shall he dwindle, peak, and pine;
Though his bark cannot be lost,
Yet it shall be tempest-tost.

Later in the play, the witches concoct a poisonous brew from all sorts of noxious substances which, with assistance from "black spirits," enables them to invoke apparitions and foresee the future – all powers that King James believed were the stuff of witchcraft.

As the years wore on, James began to have doubts about the truth of witchcraft accusations. He became aware of the political and financial use to which malicious accusations could be put, and took upon himself directly the task of exposing lies and fraud. In the light of increasing experience, he rethought his position and allowed that his earlier zeal may have been misplaced.

Once the belief had formed that diabolical practises actually took place, there remained only one problem – to find it and prove it. Such proof was, of course, not easy to find. Courts had to relax the rules of evidence to a breathtaking degree in order to secure any convictions at all. To assist prosecutors handbooks of witchcraft practises were published, the first and most influential of which was the *Malleus Maleficarum* of 1486, which laid down the ground rules for witch-hunting. Known all over mainland Europe, it contained everything a witch-hunter needed to know. It was clear that most witches were expected to be women, and a careful reader could see that under these guidelines an accusation of witchcraft would inevitably lead to a conviction. Alibis were unacceptable because a witch could easily manage simple translocation, thus being seen in more than one place at once. Confessions were taken as proof, but anyone who had practiced diabolism could not be expected to confess willingly. It was accepted that pressure would certainly be needed, and this pressure was readily applied.

In England torture was technically not a part of the judicial system, but accused witches knew that they were in for an unpleasant time. Matthew Hopkins, the infamous "Witchfinder General" between 1644 and 1646, sidestepped the rules by claiming that his methods were only persuasion. He used techniques such as sleep and food deprivation, binding his victims in painful positions for hours, and subjecting them to the humiliation of searching their bodies for the "Devil's mark" which was thought to be possessed by witches. In other countries the "persuasion" was more straightforwardly

ABOVE: The infamous *Malleus Maleficarum,* guidebook for witch prosecutors.

brutal. Torture was a crucial ingredient, not only to extract confessions, but, strangely, to "help" the accused. The inquisitors felt that suffering led to purification, a partial expiation of sin. The confessed and repentant witch could expect at least some mercy in the afterlife. The torturers thought of themselves as doing their victims a favor.

Witchcraft was not believed to be a solitary act; it involved others, and the aim of the trial would be to extract from each confessed witch the names of accomplices. Thus the pattern was established – someone was accused, and then tortured until they confessed and named others. These were in turn accused and tortured and the process repeated itself. Various other "trials" for witchcraft were devised, but they all

RIGHT: Matthew Hopkins, surrounded by witches and their familiars.

ABOVE: These French illustrations show the lengths to which the witchfinders would go to extract proof of witchcraft.

had the same unfortunate effect for the accused. An innocent verdict could only be proved by her death such as in the "swimming" trial. If she floated when bound and thrown into water, it was proof of witchcraft. If she sank and drowned, then she was innocent – but dead, anyway. A completely circular system of reasoning was thus set up. Once the basic belief in the existence of witches was accepted, there was no way to prove or disprove it. If the accusers arrived at a woman's door (almost 90 per cent of convicted witches were female), her fate was sealed. These were some of the trial procedures recommended by French jurist Jean Bodin in his *Demonomania of Witches*, 1580: "The names of all informers are to be kept secret. Children are to be forced to testify against their parents ... suspicion is sufficient ground for torture ... A person once accused must never be acquitted, unless the falsity of the accuser ... is clearer than the light of day. No punishment is too cruel for witches, including hot irons to their flesh. The judge who does not roundly execute a convicted witch should himself be put to death . . . Better to burn the innocent than let one guilty witch escape."

Given instructions like those it is easy to see how, once an area entered the grip of a witchcraze, there was very little way of stopping its momentum. As long as each confessor was required to name her fellow witches, the accusations could continue indefinitely. As long as no further proof was required and public discussion and fear

RIGHT: Witches
burning in Derneburg,
Germany, in 1555.

RIGHT: Witches
burning in Derneburg,
Germany, in 1555.

Ψ   Ψ

was constantly agitated by the detailed disclosures, the cycle could repeat itself until
there was no one left to accuse. Indeed this very nearly happened in central
Germany in 1585 when the Archbishop Elector of Trier led his region in a fanatical
witch-hunt during which two villages found themselves with only one female left
alive. It was the Catholic regions of Germany which saw the most violent and
extreme manifestations of the witchcraze. Whole areas were devastated; some officials were responsible for mass executions and individual tallies of 600, 700 and 900
dead witches were declared. During the 1620s Bishop Philipp Adolf von Ehrenberg
executed several hundred people including his own nephew and several young children as well as 19 Catholic priests. During the same period the Archbishop Elector
of Cologne oversaw the execution in Bonne of almost the entire family and office
staff of his Chancellor. It is impossible to overestimate the effect of these slaughters
on a community; when large numbers of witches were burned on the same day all
the nearby buildings were coated with human fat, and there was no escaping the
hideous nature of the whole event.

Even given the self-generating nature of the accusations and trials, we have to ask
how quite so many people could have been persuaded to join in the deadly charade.
There is not a scrap of evidence that any of the accusations or confessions were true,
or that any of the scenes described by the tortured and terrified victims took place.

The confessions were remarkably uniform and the details closely matched those
given in the handbooks, but this was hardly surprising given their wide circulation.
The *Malleus Maleficarum* went through 32 editions and was common knowledge,
and there were numerous other publications of a similar nature. A detailed account
of the trial of the North Berwick witches had been published, and transcripts of most
major trials were easily available. These accounts disclosed a wealth of information,
so that accused witches under torture could readily reel off the expected details.
Sometimes jailers sold women under torture details to include in their confessions (if
the confession did not sound convincing enough, the victim was accused of holding
back and was returned by the court for more torture), and even lists of names that

the prosecutors would be expecting to hear. As with so many things, publicity led to even greater accusations and concern. In 1612 Salazar, a lawyer and diplomat appointed to the Basque witch-craft tribunal in France, was a steadfast voice of reason, advising silence and dis-cretion to judges and churchmen and maintaining that, "It is harmful to air these matters in public at all."

Most confessions show evidence of hysteria, delusion, and hallucination, and the powerful atmosphere of fear, obsession, and religious fervor cannot be underestimated. The most infamous of the American trials showed how easily these emotions could take over. Witchcraft beliefs had been slow to take root in the American colonies and the most extreme literature, that written by Cotton Mather, was not published until five years after the last witch had been executed in England in 1684. A few cases, with their subsequent hangings, had taken place in the years since the 1640s, but they faded into insignifi-

ABOVE: Torture instruments, routinely used for the interro-gation of witches at Bamberg, Germany.

cance beside the traumatic events which took place in Salem, Massachusetts in 1692. The beginnings of unrest had begun to spread among the young girls of the strictly Puritan Salem community. Fits of agitation, overexcitement, and screaming led to convulsions and hysterics which, for want of any other diagnosis, was attributed to their being bewitched.

Prompted by questioning, the girls initially named three women as the witches responsible: a poor woman who sometimes begged, an elderly invalid, and a black servant. These accusations conformed exactly to the stereotypes of witches docu-mented by nearly 200 years of persecution throughout Europe. But, through a com-bination of blinkered credulity and uncritical zeal, in the end over 150 people were arrested. They included many totally implausible victims, convicted on flimsy evi-dence extracted under torture.

Looking now at these trials, the evident triumph of hysteria is shocking; the unsupported testimony of a confused and exhausted seven-year-old for instance, was enough to condemn her mother to death. John Willard, the deputy constable who made the first arrests, saw the dreadful way in which the affair was developing and tried to call a halt, only to be arrested, tried and hanged himself. The hunt progressed as far as the Reverend George Burroughs, who was accused of witchcraft by six of the girls. Their accusations became wilder and more incredible as they vied with each other in their evidence. The court duly convicted him, and he was executed.

LEFT: A scene in court
during the trial at
Salem, Massachusetts.

LEFT: The building in Bamberg, Germany, from where the witch-hunts were directed by the Prince-Bishops.

Of course there were people who, even in such a climate, simply did not believe that women flew on broomsticks, had orgies with the Devil, and ate babies but few spoke up. Partly this was because scepticism brought accusations down on them too. John Willard paid the price for unguarded remarks during the Salem trials, and Johannes Junius had earlier made the same discovery in Germany. He was a Burgomaster in Bamberg, where the Prince-Bishop, Johann Georg II, was conducting a murderous witch-hunting campaign (featuring a specially built "witch-house," complete with torture chambers) which resulted in the deaths of more than 600 people. Junius, appalled by these events, ventured to protest and was himself arrested and accused. After prolonged torture he confessed to witchcraft and was executed. Before he died he wrote a letter to his daughter, one of the most moving and revealing documents of the witchcraze era.

Many hundred thousand good-nights, dearly beloved daughter Veronica. Innocent have I come into prison, innocent have I been tortured, innocent I must die. For whoever comes into the witch prison must become a witch or be tortured until he invents something out of his head and – God pity him- bethinks him of something … The executioner came – God in highest heaven have mercy – and put the thumb-screws on me, both hands bound together, so that the blood ran out of the nails and everywhere, so that for four weeks I could not use my hands, as you can see from the writing … When at last the executioner led me back into the prison, he said to me "Sir, I beg you, for God's sake confess something, whether it be true or not. Invent something, for you cannot endure the torture you will be put to, and, even if you bear it all you will not escape … but one torture will follow another until you say you are a witch." And so I made my confession, but it was all a lie … Then I had to tell what people I had seen at the witch sabbat. I said I had not recognized them. So he said: "Take one street after another; begin at the market, go out on one street and back on the next." I had to name several persons there. . . And thus continuously they asked me on all the streets, though I could not and would not say more. So they gave me to the executioner, told him to strip me, shave me all over and put me to the torture. Now, dear child, you have all my confession, for which I must die. And they are sheer lies and inventions, so help me God. For all this I was forced to say through fear of the torture which was threatened beyond what I had already endured. I have taken several days to write this; my hands are both lame. I am in a sad plight. . . Good night, for your father Johannes Junius will never see you more. July 14, 1628.

Although we find it hard to accept that a rational person could accept these events, rationality hardly came into it. Witchcraft was a belief – and the role of the Devil was declared by the Church. Not to believe in it was heresy. If the belief was accepted, then there was nothing irrational about the trials themselves. For people who believed in covens, Devils and flying witches the trials brought few inconsistencies. As the belief waned, it became acceptable to condemn the trials and even to ridicule the belief itself. All societies hold beliefs in things they cannot prove, and such beliefs are often slow to change. Once they have changed it is easy to be incredulous.

WHO WERE THE WITCHES?

It is now clear that the victims of the witchcraze were not practicing anything – the accusations against them had no basis in reality. The witches were accused, not on account of their imaginary crimes but on quite different criteria. The obvious candidates, the "wise women," were sometimes scapegoated, but the pattern of accusations was much more wide-ranging.

Many accusations were political, particularly those against men or the wives of prominent men. In the later stages of the witchcraze an increasing number of these accusations were made against powerful families. Witches' property was confiscated, which was an inducement to single out wealthier figures, and among the less well-off, many old scores were settled; resentments which had simmered for years boiled over into accusations. The most striking feature of these centuries, however, is that the witches were, overwhelmingly, women.

There are several reasons for this. To begin with, they were easy targets. Women had less direct power than men. They had little control of property, land, or influence, and were tacitly expected to make use of more indirect means of control. Many women were desperately poor and supplemented their meagre diet by selling small items door to door, or begging. The affluent feared the resentment of lone women reduced to this state – it was easy for those who had withheld help to imagine that a meanly treated beggar would wish them harm, and they were always the first to be suspected when things went wrong. Today's Halloween Trick or Treaters are echoing this ancient pattern: refuse a beggar and something unpleasant may happen to you .

Most important, though, was the attitude of the Church, which was deeply misogynistic. Women were perceived as more fallible than men. Men were made in

110

ABOVE: A medieval illustration shows the agents of good and evil struggling for the soul of a young woman.

God's image, but St Augustine declared that this was not the case with women, whose bodies exposed them to temptations. They were far more susceptible than men to the persuasions of the Devil. The *Malleus Malificarum* stated unequivocally that women were dangerous, "a necessary evil, a natural temptation . . . an evil of nature painted with fair colours." This unpleasant document, with its reccurent theme of fear of and disgust for the female sex, is little more than a diatribe against women. It was a fair reflection of the thinking in the higher echelons of the Church: women were the weak link in the struggle against the Devil. This sentiment was echoed by James I, who explained that female witches outnumbered males by twenty to one because of their tendency, illustrated by the Fall in the Garden of Eden, to believe the words of the Devil.

The scale and nature of the accusations against women revealed a more general and deep-seated fear of the female sex which has not been satisfactorily explained. Women were thought to have voracious appetites – Robert Burton spoke in 1621 in his *Anatomy of Melancholy* of "women's unnatural, insatiable lust," which made them easy prey to the Devil's blandishments. Contemporary artists frequently portrayed witches' activities as erotic and their relationship with the Devil as blatantly carnal. Confessions required detailed accounts of the supposed sexual nature of the witches' crimes, such as that extracted from Walpurga Hausmannin, a German midwife from Dillingen, who in 1587 described having intercourse with the Devil and an animal familiar, as well as the usual catalogue of child murder and night flying. These accounts were delivered after the most brutally sadistic torture, performed by men and combining extreme physical pain with the humiliation of stripping and detailed physical examination. The sexual nature of witch interrogations leads us to question the true motives of the inquisitors but does not resolve the question of why such levels of aggression against women were accepted during this period.

Recent historians have suggested that the arenas of witchcraft crimes were chiefly domestic and thus in female jurisdiction, closely bound up with women's work in the spheres of food, children, and animals. But this does not explain why these accusations, which were entirely fictitious anyway, should have been brought in the first place. Another suggestion is that women in the Western tradition are more closely associated with informal aspects of religion – the more powerful, if less controllable, aspects such as prophesy, trance and healing – and this would make them more obvious choices for diabolical activities. Whatever the truth of these possibilities, it is interesting that as the witchcraze spiralled, the chain of accusations began to include men – and prominent men at that. At this point, towards the end of the 17th century, the bubble burst; the whole business began to seem incredible, and the craze gently wound down.

As with many historical movements, however, there were violent outbreaks just before the end; these may have been just the thing to convince those who were beginning to have doubts. In Britain, the self-styled "Witchfinder General," Matthew Hopkins, embarked on a reign of terror which resulted in the trial and execution of at least 230 people in 1645-6. As his brutal and ruthless methods progressed, admiration turned to revulsion, and his rise in wealth, status, and power caused growing opposition. Contemporary woodcuts show the witchfinder being paid his money in the shadow of hanged witches, and accounts reveal how sickened local people were by his activities. His retreat from the scene, and subsequent death, marked the turn of the tide in England.

Still later, in 1692, the Salem trials were the turning-point for America. Hysteria, cruelty and bigotry were so clearly displayed that there must inevitably have been a taking stock afterwards. In 1696 some of the jurors who sat in the Salem trial issued a *Confession of Error*: "Whereby we fear . . . we have been instrumental with others, though ignorantly and unwittingly, to bring upon ourselves and this people of the Lord the guilt of innocent blood . . . we do therefore signify . . . our deep sense of, and sorrow for our errors . . . we were sadly deluded and mistaken, for which we are much disquieted and distressed in our minds . . . we would none of us do such things again on such grounds for the whole world."

AFTER THE WITCHCRAZE

Isolated cases of simple sorcery continued to appear, much as they always had done, as in the case of Ursula Clarke of Dunstable in England, who was charged in 1667 with trying to bring about the death of a man by cursing. As late as the 1850s the Bishop of Orleans, France, reported that "wise women" and local charmers could still be found in the French countryside, but devil-worshipping witches had effectively vanished from public consciousness. Interest in the supernatural remained as strong as ever – there were cases of demonic possession, and black magic – but witchcraft had dropped from the official language. The intellectual elite had ceased to believe in it, and there was an air of embarrassment about the whole episode. The French philosopher Descartes (1596-1650) had asserted that belief in devils had no basis in reason, and those who were now perceiving the beginnings of the new liberalism of thought in western Europe were anxious not to identify with what had now become superstition. In 1654 the French writer Cyrano de Bergerac published *A Letter Against Witches* which poured scorn and derision upon those foolish enough to believe such fantasies. A powerful movement involving hundreds of thousands of people over almost 300 years ended rapidly and quietly, amid jokes and disclaimers.

As in Europe, there followed a phase in which accusations of witchcraft simply became inappropriate. Elements of the witchcraze beliefs lingered in some corners of both America and Europe, although they were not widely acted upon. In this century rural areas of Germany have experienced unpleasant outbreaks of witchcraft accusations based on alleged cooperation with the Devil, amid claims that

RIGHT: The Dropping
Well at
Knaresborough,
Yorkshire in the north
of England. Mother
Shipton was a well-
known wise woman
who presided over the
well, continuing a
tradition which
survived the
witchcraze.

RIGHT: The Dropping
Well at
Knaresborough,
Yorkshire in the north
of England. Mother
Shipton was a well-
known wise woman
who presided over the
well, continuing a
tradition which
survived the
witchcraze.

OPPOSITE: Witches
became ambivalent
figures in folklore and
fairy tales during the
18th and 19th
centuries. This is the
witch from Hans
Christian Andersen's
The Snow Queen,
written in 1872.

these communities have never lost their belief in diabolical witchcraft. In 1976, a suspected witch in a small German village suffered severe burns and the loss of all her property when neighbours burned her house. *Hexenbanner* (or witch-hunters) can still be found, diagnosing witchcraft, detecting witches, and supplying remedies. As late as 1977, a new edition of an 18th-century *grimoire* (magical handbook) appeared, offering advice and practical steps for those being bewitched. This apparent survival was, however, the exception. Elsewhere, charmers and magical healers still existed and sorcery and magic continued, as it had always done, but the connection with the Devil had evaporated. No more is heard about Satan's crusade to take over the hearts and minds of women. The war between Catholic and Protestant resolves into a decision to coexist, and the heat is suddenly gone from hellfire.

No one can say definitively why the ruling elite (for the witchcraze was never a folk movement) decided to drop the diabolical connection. But as their outlook moved toward the scientific positivism of the 18th century scheming devils and flying witches became an illogical illusion, and folk beliefs about magic settled back into their previous low-key pattern. With the developing interest in medicine, illness was now more likely to be accorded a natural explanation than attributed to the resentment of others. A flourishing Church had the answer to fate; the will of God, often mysterious, determined all outcomes, and misfortunes must be accepted with fortitude and faith.

For 100 years there was very little reference to witches. But with the arrival of the 19th century the exoticism of witches and high magic began once more to capture the educated imagination. In 1830 the Scottish novelist, Sir Walter Scott, published

Ψ   Ψ

ABOVE: The frontispiece from a magical handbook used by wiccans at the beginning of the 20th century.

Letters on Demonology which made the occult an acceptable topic for discussion. Charles Leland's *Aradia*, a supposedly accurate account of Italian witchcraft, was published in 1899 to considerable interest. Cults and societies with mystical overtones, such as the Rosicrucians – a secret order claiming to have originated with the mystical scholars of the Pharaoh Thutmose III in 1489 BC – grew in popularity as the century wore on. At the turn of the century Aleister Crowley and Macgregor Mathers, both members of a secret society called the Hermetic Order of the Golden Dawn, declared themselves dedicated practitioners of the occult and claimed to be able to conjure spirits and even the Devil himself. Although scandal and public condemnation surrounded these dabblings, they were a sign that a new occult movement was beginning.

Interest in the supernatural continued throughout the 19th and early 20th centuries but it was only after World War II that the word "witchcraft" began cautiously to appear in fashionable occult circles. In the 1950s Gerald Gardner, an ex-customs officer in the Far East, proclaimed that on his return to England he had been initiated as a witch; he maintained that witchcraft was alive and well and had survived in secret. Gardner had written a fictional account of these ideas, *High Magic's Aid*, which created a stir of interest. Although he was influenced by the high magic of Aleister Crowley (a form of ceremonial magic directed more toward mystical and spiritual enlightenment than pragmatism), the new witchcraft he created was firmly in the folk tradition, accessible to ordinary people and increasingly adapted to practical use. Many of his claims, such as the authenticity of his early accounts, were later discounted. Nevertheless, inspired by the enthusiastic response of his group of followers, Gardner used his research into the past to design ceremonies and rituals for the modern witch. They were published in a book entitled *Witchcraft Today* which sold widely. The movement grew and spread, with small groups springing up across the world. Different interpretations meant that there was little uniformity among the covens and no overall organization. The freedom and individuality which modern witches value acts against their becoming a unified and recognizable group.

Today's witch is more likely to be young and prosperous than old and poor. The possibility of malevolence has previously been fundamental to the definition, in whatever culture or time, yet there are now numbers of "white" witches whose aims seem entirely benign. Although modern witches are sometimes secretive and nervous of being mistaken for Devil worshippers or child abusers, most of them feel able to discuss their beliefs. They are not outcasts or scapegoats, although they do experience prejudice and considerable opposition from Christian groups. As in the past, anyone claiming a power to help is naturally suspected of being able to cause harm.

Modern witches are concerned with fulfiling the potential of the human mind. They believe that the ritual and magical paraphernalia of their cere-

LEFT: Dr Gerald Gardner, who amalgamated folk traditions with high magic to create the basis of modern witchcraft.

monies serves to open the mind and allow its hidden powers to work. There may be spells and bindings, but the ultimate objective is self-realization rather than humble magic. American groups in particular stress the union with nature and the earth, and see "The Craft" as a vehicle through which to gain psychic balance and power. Ritual is an important part of the new witchcraft, and here at least is a clear link with witches of other times and places. Whether the Craft is practiced in groups (covens) or alone there are precise ceremonies to follow. The fact of their recent origin does not detract from their effect, or the feeling that they are timeless.

This is modern witchcraft responding to modern needs. In the general vacuum of belief that characterizes the societies in which today's practitioners live, they have found a way to address today's problems and concerns in a spiritual manner. In rejecting the religious traditions of their cultures they are bypassing history and reaching back to a simpler (if mythical) past where power and control seemed more directly available to the individual. By combining the subversion of prevailing wisdom with the maximization of personal power these groups resemble both medieval European witches and the witches of non-industrial societies all over the world. The defining details always vary, as each culture demands its own responses. But every society has its witches, and it is as true now as it ever was – there may be one living next door to you.

CHAPTER VI

THINKING WITH MONSTERS

ABOVE: The Loch Ness Monster breaking the surface of the water – the photograph that once convinced the world.

or many people the 1994 disclosure that the first eerie picture of the Loch Ness Monster was a simple fake brought a twinge of disappointment. Against all the odds, we want to keep alive the possibility that there is something there. In fact the revelation has done little to deter the investigators of the mystery, or the 500,000 visitors who annually visit the Scottish loch to stare into its dark depths and imagine its unknown, monstrous inhabitant. Nessie, as the monster is affectionately known (and many monsters do have pet names) is one of the numerous quasi-mythological creatures about which stories continually circulate. These creatures are quite different from known animals or humans and possess characteristics which would seem to make their existence impossible; yet there are always witnesses who have seen them, and many more who know someone else who has.

Twentieth-century Westerners may consider themselves too sophisticated to believe in monsters, but such myths still capture the public imagination. Monsters are good box office; the classic stories keep turning up, with Dracula and Frankenstein movies repeatedly being remade to express contemporary interpretations of well-known themes. We may know that monsters do not really exist, but we are keen to consider the prospect of them in art, literature and drama.

Humans have always speculated on the existence of beings which straddle the worlds of the mundane and the supernatural; which may, as well as being physically extraordinary, have supernatural powers. In mythology, fabulous beasts such as dragons not only fly and breathe fire but intervene in the lives of men and women with magical effect.

ABOVE: Travellers' Tales - a 1499 illustration of the monsters which an explorer could expect to encounter abroad.

RIGHT: Monsters capture the public imagination. Here the Loch Ness Monster, always regarded with affection, is portrayed as friendly and appealing.

Ψ

DOMENICA DEL CORRIERE

Anno 63 - N. 32 - L. 40   *Settimanale del* **CORRIERE DELLA SERA**   6 Agosto 1961

È tornato il mostro di Lochness? Uno scolaretto di Edimburgo, mentre si trovava sulle rive del lago scozzese, famoso per le frequenti e periodiche apparizioni del favoloso animale, giura di aver visto affiorare uno strano bestione. Gli porse la mela che aveva in mano. Il mostro stava per addentarla, ma poi, spaventato da un rumore sospetto, si tuffò e sparì sott'acqua. (Dis. di W. Molino). Vedi servizio a pagg. 14 e 15.

La ragazza venuta da lontano

Il giallo di Hitchcock - a pagg. 6 e 7

Ψ

119

ABOVE: The Garden of Eden, part of the creation myth of the Judeo-Christian religions. Each society has its own account of its origins.

It is useful to think of myths as tools; things to think with rather than ends in themselves. The German theologian Bartsch defined myth in 1953 as "the expression of unobservable realities in terms of observable phenomena" and we must regard myths as coded messages; the literal truth, interesting as it may be, is less important than the questions and possible answers that the myth provides. Not believing in the actual events of the Garden of Eden would not make the Book of Genesis irrelevant.

Every culture has myths which deal with the eternal questions of our nature and origins; Genesis is the creation myth of Judeo-Christian societies. Anthropologists have found that myths have a common structural language. They deal with pairs of opposing elements, such as life and death, male and female, our people and the rest, good and evil, God and man, constantly restating the categories whereby we make sense of the world. Genesis, through repeated illustrations of such oppositions, tells us that humans are God's highest creation, equipped with knowledge, the capacity for thought and the consciousness of good and evil. We are set apart from animals, and set apart from God, and must establish relations with both in the consciousness of our separation. Whether there were really two people and a serpent in a garden is not vital to the central message of the myth. Similarly, debating the existence of Nessie is diverting but beside the point; the monster's importance lies in making us think about a power in nature that we still cannot completely comprehend. We strive to improve our scientific knowledge but the animal world may still have a few surprises for us – one of them possibly right there in Loch Ness.

LEFT: The Blackfoot of North America were traditionally dependent on the buffalo. Their mythology reflects a close concern with the delicate relationship between human society and the natural world.

Much of our myth-telling focuses on the boundaries between animals and humans, and many of our fantastic creatures are variations on animals we know. The relationship is necessarily ambivalent; we have always recognized that we are animals with animal natures, but know ourselves to be crucially different. Our special human qualities must be defined and the lines drawn. The relationship may often be warm but it is significant that to call someone "an animal" is to deliver an insult. With this goes the inescapable fact that we have always killed animals for food and used the animal world in various ways for our comfort, convenience, and survival.

Many societies, especially hunting societies, have strong animal mythologies in which the human and animal worlds overlap. The Native American Plains Indians had complex myths involving the buffalo, upon which they depended for food. In these myths the buffalo and the Indians once communicated in human terms and laid down the rules by which necessary hunting could take place in an atmosphere of mutual respect. A Blackfoot myth tells how the buffalo taught the people a ritual dance and song which would restore to life the creatures killed for food. The Blackfoot placed the knowledge of this ritual in the keeping of the men's associations, which had the responsibility of maintaining the harmonious relationship between the hunters and the hunted, and thus the survival of the group. The animals are seen as bestowing life and even social rules upon humans. The central North American Dakota have a myth in which they were given maize by the buffalo. Appearing first as a beautiful young girl, the buffalo gave the humans a pipe and some maize and taught them how to use them. She also gave them rules for living and vital rituals to perform before turning, in front of their eyes, into a buffalo calf. Every time the myth is told and the rituals performed the Dakota are invited to consider that animals are not just dumb creatures to be slaughtered at will; they have a superior wisdom and have given humans the guidelines for their society.

WEREWOLVES

Ψ Ψ

Despite, or perhaps because of, their perceived interdependence with animals, humans have always been concerned with maintaining a separation, cherishing their distinctness from the rest of the animal world. Anything which blurs the categories of man and animal is unsettling and threatening. The problems of the human – animal boundary are focused most clearly in stories of creatures who are a mixture of both. Such hybrid creatures change from one state to the other, and are difficult to detect in either. They seem to embrace the worst characteristics of both worlds, and are objects of both fear and repulsion. The ability to change shape has always been connected with the forces of evil; 16th-century European witches were thought to change into animals at their covens, and traditional American Navajos felt that any coyote, bear, or owl seen at night could well be a witch or sorcerer going about their evil work.

The best animal candidates for hybrids are the very opposite of the civilized human. We have speech, cut our hair and nails, wear clothes and attempt to control the violent and sexual sides of our nature. The howling, hairy, sharp-clawed wolf has always been portrayed as frightening, ferocious, and gratuitously violent, an unnerving but ideal partner in a metamorphosis which forces us to consider the boundaries. Recent books and television documentaries have attempted to rehabilitate the wolf, revealing it to be a peaceable, social animal, killing only to eat; but its image remains tarnished. The wolf howl is still the sound signature for ghost and horror movies. Wherever there are wolves there are wolf-man monsters which we call werewolves ("were" from the Old English word for "man"). Where there are no wolves another were-animal is feared: were-lions in Africa, were-jaguars in South America and were-tigers in India.

For most of us, our notions of werewolves are formed by the movies. The

RIGHT: A 16th-century woodcut showing a man attacked by a werewolf. Europe was prone to constant werewolf scares at this time.

transformation of man to wolf has challenged special-effects technicians to their most ingenious efforts. Although based on folklore, myth, and the recorded cases of those actually convicted of lycanthropy (wolf-man transformation), film images owe much to the imagination of the directors. To get to grips with werewolves, we need to go a little further back.

The wolf-man motif is ancient, and legend and folklore are rich in werewolf tales. The 1st-century Roman writer Petronius narrates in *Satyricon* a werewolf story complete with all the classic details: moonlight, the removal of human clothes, and the transformation to blood-lusting wolf terrorizing the countryside. In the 5th century, the Greek writer Herodotus quotes Scythian villagers who tell of their neighbours' annual transformation into wolves. In subsequent centuries, wolves themselves were seen as a more serious problem. Sheep farming grew in importance to humans, but unfortunately lambs were tempting food for wolves. Forested areas, the wolves' breeding grounds, increased and during the Middle Ages wolves became well-established nuisances. As late as 1420 they could still be spotted on the edges of Paris. In England, hunting made the wolf extinct by 1500, and a little later in Scotland, Wales, and Ireland. In continental Europe, especially eastern Europe, where there were wilder areas for the wolf to retreat to, the problem was more intractable. Public fear of the animals sparked werewolf reports, which ebbed and flowed through Europe along with the size of the wolf population.

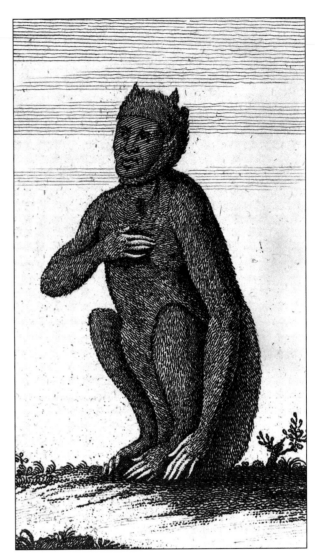

ABOVE: Were-animals do not have to be wolves, although they are the most common. This 18th-century illustration shows a were- or man-tiger.

The perception of werewolves has altered over time. The oldest references do not suggest the same level of fear and loathing as later accounts, although in his *Satyricon* Petronius's storyteller relates that after identifying a werewolf he "could never eat a bit of bread with him, no, if you'd have killed me." But in general, classical times' treatment of werewolves was fairly matter-of-fact; they were merely identified and obliged to pay compensation for their damage.

During the Middle Ages, however, werewolves were becoming something of a scourge in Europe. They were thought to come about both by accident and by design. Those unfortunate enough to be conceived under a full moon would certainly become one; sleeping out under a full moon could be dangerous, too. Sharing drinking water with wolves might do it. One could become a werewolf as the result of a curse, and there was a strong belief that the condition was hereditary. The 16th-century Swiss philosopher and physician Paracelsus thought that werewolves were the returned souls of particularly unpleasant men. Aspects of physical appearance,

ABOVE: **This drawing shows the overlapping of human and animal characteristics which makes the werewolf so disturbing.**

particularly excessive hairyness or a loping gait, could lead to suspicions of being a werewolf. It was felt that some individuals actively wanted to experience the night-time freedom to hunt and attack and there were magical procedures for those who wanted to become werewolves. These involved the removing of clothes, chanting in magic circles, and donning wolf-fur belts and masks.

Whether the transformation was accidental or deliberate, it occurred only during the hours of darkness, often only at full moon, and involved the hunting, killing, and eating, not only of animals but also of people. The victims tended also to be female and young, and were sexually violated during the attack. The most reprehensible deeds of humans – murder, rape, and cannibalism – were committed in wolf form. If medieval werewolves were captured they reverted to human form, when they were usually killed. Sometimes they could be cured, especially if they were involuntary werewolves, by losing three drops of blood or being called by their name while in wolf form. Various talismans, such as yew or ash branches, could afford protection if all else failed, but on the whole little could be done to stop the werewolves.

In view of the unpleasant habits of werewolves the medieval attitude was remarkably benign. Typical was a 12th-century story by Marie de France, Lai de Bisclavret, which tells of a lady in Brittany who discovers that her husband is a werewolf. She arranges the theft of his clothes when he is out in wolf form, knowing that he cannot resume his human shape without them. A suitable time after his mysterious disappearance she marries another knight. The husband, trapped as a wolf, attracts the king's attention and returns to the court, where he manages to cast suspicion on the wife and her new husband, who eventually admit their guilt. The clothes are retrieved, the knight resumes his form and is restored to his position, while his plotting wife is cast out.

Such a story would have been inconceivable during the 16th- and 17th-century witchcraze in Europe, when the perception of werewolves took a more sinister turn. Wolves became associated with the Devil and werewolves were thought to be witches who, in accordance with their Satanic pact, turned into wolves and spent the night committing mayhem. In this shape they would attend sabbats; some werewolves were thought to be demons themselves. Not all werewolves practiced other forms of witchcraft – many were thought to have made the pact just for the power to assume wolf form and commit the most evil crimes imaginable. In the fevered search for the Devil which gripped Europe during this time there were plenty of instances of lycanthropy linked to witchcraft. In France in 1570 Gilles Garnier, a poor recluse, was accused by villagers after several wolf attacks on children in the region around Dole. Witnesses to one attack apparently recognized his features in the attacking

wolf. Gilles was arrested and tortured, after which he confessed in detail to the attacks and to eating the flesh of previous victims. He was sentenced to be burned at the stake. A whole family of werewolves, the Gandillons, was arrested and executed in the Jura region of France in 1598, again on the basis of their own confessions. One brother descibed how "Satan clothed them in a wolf's skin . . . and they went on all fours and ran about the country."

Eye-witnesses claimed to have seen the transformation in the case of Peter Stubbe, a German tried in 1589. Known across Europe as the werewolf of Cologne, Stubbe became a household name, and the details of his case supplied much of the material for subsequent accusations in other areas. For years his neighbourhood had been troubled by murderous sexual attacks on women and girls. A werewolf was suspected, and during one chase it was sighted. Suddenly Stubbe appeared in normal human form and the pursuers were sure they had seen him abandon his wolf belt (obtained during his earlier pact with the Devil) in order to escape capture by their dogs. The villagers did not need much convincing that they had their werewolf; Stubbe had committed incest with his daughter and sister and was known for his voracious sexual appetite. It was assumed that he had made his Satanic pact in order to pursue his dreadful inclinations more freely, and after his capture he was tortured and executed. Such cases inevitably kept the werewolf idea alive. As with other forms of witchcraft accusations, people soon became aware of the shocking details, which torture elicited from the suspects. But as the witchcraze waned, so did the accusations of lycanthropy, and it was thought naive to accuse people of turning into wolves. By the late 1600s only the crimes of attacking and murdering could be tried

ABOVE: A 1590 woodcut of the sequence of events leading up to the death of the convicted German werewolf Peter Stubbe.

Ψ

Ψ

in court; werewolves were held to be an illusion, and thus not admissible.

Although werewolves disappeared from the courts they had not, of course, vanished from folk memory. When Gevaudan, an area of central southern France, began to suffer wolf attacks at the end of the 18th century the ferocity and daring of the assaults revived the werewolf fear. About 50 people were thought to have been killed by a bloodthirsty, wolf-like monster. "The Bête de Gevaudon" was seen by many witnesses, who commented on its human characteristics, but although the stories persisted and rumours abounded the perpetrator was never apprehended. The attacks were later attributed to a wandering pack of wolves, but the eye-witness accounts remained unexplained.

During the 19th century wolf hunts effectively wiped out the wolf population of France, and attacks both by real wolves and werewolves gradually diminished. There have been various attempts to explain werewolf beliefs and their tenacity, but they have only offered partial and unsatisfactory hypotheses. The occurrences have been dismissed as a form of mental illness which prompted persecution of its sufferers. Certainly some people do believe themselves to be werewolves and try to act accordingly; this has always been acknowledged, and lycanthropy is one of the oldest psychiatric diagnoses. Peter Stubbe may well have been a psychopathic serial killer with cannibalistic urges. Other medical explanations have been put forward, from ergot poisoning to porphyria and rabies, but although they may go some way to explaining certain aspects of werewolf incidents, medical diagnoses fail to address the question of why humans persist in their interest in such an unlikely event as a man or woman turning into a wolf. The answer must lie in what the werewolf myth does to help us define ourselves; the notion of werewolves speaks mainly about the dark side of human nature, the ferocious flouting of our civilized rules by the barbaric elements lurking in human society. Werewolves are repellent, frightening, yet eternally fascinating.

Ψ  Ψ

SASQUATCH, BIGFOOT, AND YETI

With the gradual driving out of wild animals from the inhabited parts of the world, modern society has turned to the remaining wilderness areas to find signs of other sorts of monster hybrids. It is not surprising that explorers of icy wastes, deep oceans and dense jungles return with stories of strange beasts; not just undiscovered species but huge, semi-human monsters with the will and the strength to attack. Media stories feed a fascinated audience and little by little it becomes accepted that there must be something there.

The Native Americans of Canada's north-west coast tell ancient stories of the sasquatch, a tall, two-legged, ape-like creature. Its existence in the area was confirmed at the end of the 19th century by gold-miners, who reported meeting the giant ape-man and barely escaping with their lives. Similar types of beast have emerged all down the west coast of the Americas, earlier American Indian stories being reinforced by 20th-century descriptions.

BELOW: Over 16 inches (40cm) long, this strange footprint raised the possibility of a bigfoot creature in Washington State, USA in 1969.

A recent spate of bigfoot hunting began in 1958 in the western United States when giant footprints were discovered near a construction site. The prints indicated a creature of considerably more weight and height than a human and aroused instant media attention. Brief sightings were reported, but nothing substantial until 1967 when two bigfoot hunters were riding, miles from roads or habitation, in northern California. They knew that tracks had been seen in the area, but were unprepared for the sudden sight of a 10ft-tall (3m) ape-like creature walking calmly away while observing them over its shoulder. One of the men, Roger Patterson, grabbed his movie camera and managed to film the creature, and this footage remains the most compelling piece of evidence in the bigfoot mystery. Experts declare that the film itself has not been tampered with, which leaves the possibility that the figure itself was faked, either by Patterson and his friend, or by others pulling a hoax. It seems unlikely that it could have been a hoax of which Patterson and Gimlin were unaware, as they were in a remote area and not following a planned route; the hoax would have been impossible to set up, and too dangerous. Gimlin was armed with a powerful hunting rifle, and there would have been a substantial risk of him firing at the bigfoot. Even assuming the pair's collusion, it is hard to prove that the bigfoot on the film is a fake. Biomechanical scientists point out that the gait of the creature is consistent with its size, is completely natural and unforced, and is not that of a man dressed in a large furry suit.

Inhospitable mountain slopes may not seem an ideal home for any hominid, but wandering ape-men have been spotted even on snowfields. The

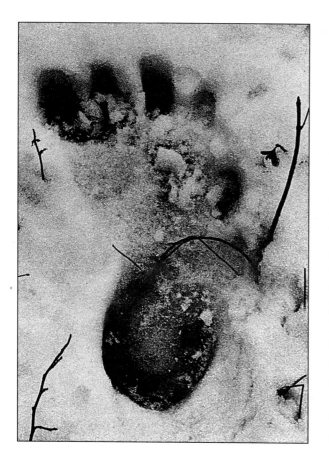

Ψ

ABOVE: A frame from Roger Patterson's film of the bigfoot at Bluff Creek.

RIGHT: Monster hunting in the Andes: an impression from the 1950s of a yeti-like creature detected by the geologist A. L. Pich.

Ψ

yeti, similar in its characteristics to the American sasquatch and bigfoot, has been familiar to native Sherpas in the Himalayas for generations. According to them, Yeti live mainly in remote valleys, venturing onto snowfields only in transit and thus not really living up to their colloquial name of "Abominable Snowman." Sherpas are familiar with the wandering creatures who sometimes approach the fringes of villages to attack its weaker members. As late as 1913 a sherpa girl was said to have been carried away by a yeti and never seen again, and violent encounters are still alleged to take place in remoter areas. The yeti-hunting movement only gained real momentum when Europeans began to spend time in the area. In 1832 the British Traveller B. H. Hodson reported seeing a large, long-haired, ape-like animal walking on its hind legs. In 1921 a team surveying the slopes of Mount Everest saw large, dark figures moving across the landscape and found enormous footprints in the snow. From then on mountaineering teams produced sightings thick and fast. Research among the local inhabitants revealed that sherpas were not only certain of the yeti's existence but could distinguish between different types, classified by size, shape, diet, and color of fur. The first photographs of yeti footprints appeared in

1951; they were taken by a well-known mountaineer, Eric Shipton, who followed a trail of them. Since then sightings and clues have mounted, but the conclusive proof, a skeleton or indeed a living example, has failed to materialize.

There are various possible explanations for yeti sightings. They include delusion and hallucination (possibly brought on by oxygen deprivation at high altitudes), large bears or wolves, misplaced apes, hardy hermits and, in latter years, deliberate hoaxes. Accepting that the large number of consistent sightings indicates that something is going on, scientists have sought among their theories for a further potential explanation. One recently connected these creatures to a prehistoric giant ape, Gigantopithecus, thought to have become extinct in Asia about 300,000 years ago. Fossil remains indicate that Gigantopithecus looked somewhat similar to the yeti and bigfoot, and it is speculated that, against all the odds, some members of this ape family may have survived to the present day.

Almost more interesting than the physical reality of the bigfoot is the way that tales of the wild, hairy ape-man have captured modern imaginations. Although feared for their size and power, these humanoid figures are in general sympathetically regarded, and are not seen as personifying the viler aspects of human life. The motif of the lone, untrappable figure on the very fringes of civilization has considerable appeal for the constrained members of today's society.

MERMAIDS

Not all creatures which blur the human – animal boundary are symbols of power or aggression. Most traditional societies living near the sea hold beliefs about human-like creatures which dwell beneath the waves. Most commonly, particularly in Europe, these take the shape of mermaids, creatures with the body of a woman and the tail of a fish who live beneath the sea but are drawn to the land and the world of humans. More than any other creature the mermaid portrays the tragedy of being anomalous – neither one thing nor the other. Magical beings with enviable powers, they can marry humans and have their children, but their nature remains fundamentally different. They were thought to be dangerous to sailors, less for their evil intent than for the fact that they craved human company – beneath the waves if necessary.

Christopher Columbus recorded sightings of mermaids on his 15th-century voyages, and stories about the perils of the lonely mermaid and her tempting songs were standard sailors' lore until well into the 19th century. The sightings have been explained as confusions with seals, manatees, and similar sea creatures, but the mermaid mythology must have a firmer basis than mistaken identity. The Phoenicians and Corinthians put mermaids on their coins, and accounts of mermaid encounters have come down to us from Roman times. There are stories of a mermaid captured off Ireland in 558 and another off Holland in 1403. One, named Melusine, was

ABOVE: Melusine leaving her home on land to return to the sea.

LEFT: All mermaid stories have unhappy endings - they deal with the problems of love between people from different worlds.

reputed to have actually married a relative of the French Count of Poitiers, in the Middle Ages. Descendants of the family continued to claim mermaid blood for several generations.

The French story ended, as mermaid tales tend to do, in sadness; the husband broke his word to Melusine and she had to return to the sea, grieving for her babies left behind. Mermaid stories revolve around the love between humans and mermaids, and the tales include both of the options – the mermaid coming to live on land and the man going to live beneath the sea. Inevitably problems arise: both miss their homes and family, and the arrival of children stretches the dilemma of loyalty even further. Betrayal, loss, and grief feature in the final working out of the conflict. What could be a more appropriate mythology for sailors, who voyage in the company of men into the alien, dangerous environment of the sea, and have to reconcile their lives with those of their families left behind?

ABOVE: The magically splendid world of the fairies, tucked inconspicuously away near the forest floor.

FAIRIES

Not all mythical creatures have such close human associations. They may exist in order to address our thoughts not so much to aspects of our humanity as to some other aspects of our lives with which we struggle. Life and luck are unpredictable, which may be partly due to small, capricious creatures who influence our lives for their own amusement. Fairies have been part of European belief for centuries, especially in Celtic countries. Shakespeare made use of them in his plays, and they appear widely in European literature and folk tales. Nowadays they rarely venture outside the pages of children's books, but they are still a part of modern culture.

There is no consensus on the origin of fairies, but they are generally held to be non-human spirits, always small and often with wings, who possess magical powers which they may exercise for both good and evil. There are bad fairies and good fairies, who between them can account for much variation of fortune, especially that connected with babies and children. There is a ancient belief, recounted by the 19th-century Scottish novelist Sir Walter Scott, that fairies like to kidnap babies, a calamity against which parents were vigilant from the Middle Ages to the 1800s.

Fairies live in wild areas such as woods and streams, and are closely associated with nature. They are normally invisible, except to those with clairvoyant gifts, but can make themselves known to any human if the occasion demands. But fairy and human lives have long overlapped, and the orderly and prosaic events of humans

Ψ ABOVE: The faked photograph of the
Cottingley fairies. Many were
deceived, including the writer Sir
Arthur Conan Doyle.

RIGHT: Edmund Dulac's imaginary
fairies, from the beginning of the
20th century.

have been constantly disturbed by the whimsical activities of the fairy world. Stories
hark back to an earlier age when the boundaries between the mortal and fairy worlds
were more fluid and anything, even love, was possible between them. In recent times
these worlds seem to have drawn further apart as busy, urban, modern life inter-
venes, but in many rural areas, particularly in Ireland, the world of "the little people"
is still acknowledged.

When a series of photographs of garden fairies appeared in Britain in 1917 there
was an immediate rush of interest. Two young English girls, Elsie Wright and her
sister Frances, claimed that fairies frequently visited them in their garden in
Cottingley, Yorkshire, and that they had been able to take photographs. Many people
were completely convinced by the pictures, while others enjoyed considering the
possibility that fairies really existed. One of those with no doubts was the author and
inventor of Sherlock Holmes, Sir Arthur Conan Doyle, who went so far as to write a
book, Coming of the Fairies (1922), citing the photographs as proof. Experts
denounced the photographs as fakes, although they were unable at the time to say
exactly how it was done. Conan Doyle was ridiculed for his gullability, but the photographs remained something of a mystery until the early 1980s, when the girls confessed that they had indeed faked the evidence. The photographs were genuine
enough, but the fairies were pictures stuck on card and attached to the greenery of
the garden. Despite this, both girls firmly maintained that they had been visited by
fairies, but, frustrated by being unable to photograph them, had resorted to forgery.

LEFT: The oriental dragon, an indelible symbol of awe-inspiring splendour.

ABOVE: Dragons are among our most ancient monsters. This one comes from the Ishtar Gate, Babylon.

Ψ

DRAGONS

Less affectionately regarded than fairies, but more thoroughly divorced from human characteristics, the dragon is the most widespread and familiar of the fantastic creatures. Any child in Europe, America or Asia could describe one if asked – they have scales, tails, sharp teeth and claws, frequently breathe fire and often have wings. Dragons play a part in numerous myths and represent different things, from good luck in China to a vehicle for the Devil in the Old Testament, depending on their cultural context. They are found in the most ancient Chinese art, on Persian and Syrian pottery, on the walls of Egyptian tombs and in the Bible. The word itself comes from the Greek *drakon*, meaning flashing or fiery; the Greek warrior Hercules, described by Homer, had a fearsome dragon with eyes of fire depicted on his shield.

Dragons can be helpful but are more often full of terrifying power. Their magic is strong – they can fly vast distances, change their shape and size, and cause changes in the elements. But dragons, though they command such forces, are not always very clever. They can be outwitted by humans with a combination of courage and brains.

Typically, dragons are interested in maidens and treasure. Their usual role is to guard hoards of gold and gems, often in underground lairs or caves where their scaly bulk might lie slumbering for thousands of years if necessary. From time to time, however, they need to feed – on anything from sheep to young girls. In western

cultures this nuisance needed to be addressed, providing the perfect opportunity for heroes to display their prowess. The most famous dragon-killer was St George, but it is thought that this was not the same saint who became patron saint of England. The dragon-slaying St George is more likely to have been a 4th-century bishop who was reputed to have put paid to a particularly destructive dragon in North Africa. His arrival saved the king's daughter, and his victory, which was effected with the help of faith and the Sign of the Cross, established his reputation prior to his later martyrdom. The triumph of Christianity was often an important part of dragon fighting before the Middle Ages: St Samson killed a dragon in Wales, St Philip one in Phrygia, St Florent one in the Loire region of France, and numerous other saints demonstrated the power of the Cross as they battled with the monsters.

Often the slaying of the dragon brings out qualities unsuspected by even the heroes themselves, leading to the idea that dragons may represent the constraints we put upon ourselves through greed and inertia. Typical of dragon mythology is the village held in thrall to a visiting beast, forced to give up its wealth, its food, and sometimes its women, paralyzed by fear and unable to continue its everyday life. Although the dragons appear to come from outside the society, threatening its passive population, they can be seen as a metaphor for the mean-mindedness and lack of vision which frequently afflict smaller communities. The dragon-slayers open new doors and

ABOVE LEFT: By his victory over the dragon St George ensured for himself a place in folklore for over 16 centuries.

ABOVE: An eastern European fairy-tale dragon. Many children's stories represent dragons as friendly and misunderstood.

bring in new eras of freedom, often assisted by the most innocent and unsophisticated members of the group. The stories of their exploits demonstrate what can be achieved against the monsters, once the decision to fight them has been taken.

VAMPIRES

One class of monster is regarded as unequivocally evil. Although they take human form, vampires are utterly inhuman; they are predatory travesties of real people. The defining characteristics of vampires are that they are dead, and that they rise as corpses in the night to suck the blood of the living. Blood-sucking creatures are a universal motif. The earliest known depiction of a blood-sucking human form appears on a Babylonian cylinder seal about 4,000 years old. Blood-sucking spirits and corpses occur throughout classical mythology, with accounts given by the Greek writer Apollonius and the Romans, Apuleius, Petronius, and Ovid; while similar myths occur across the Indian subcontinent and China. Malaysia has a series of beliefs focusing on childbirth; a langsuir is a woman dying in or after childbirth who returns within weeks as a flying vampire that preys upon children. A pontianak is the stillborn baby of a woman who has become a langsuir, who itself becomes a blood-sucker. Ancient Malaysian tradition used many remedies and protections to fight against these creatures; some of them still exist as superstitions in contemporary society.

The word "vampire," of Slav origin, first appeared in English in 1732 in a report on the case of the Serbian vampire Arnold Paole. Paole, an ordinary Serbian villager,

RIGHT: A recent Interview with a Vampire. Hollywood constantly remakes the classic monster films, expressing the changing viewpoints of each generation.

LEFT: The burial of a vampire, observing the traditional precautions.

Ψ

had returned from a tour of army duty in Greece strangely disquieted. Eventually he revealed to his wife that he had been bitten by a vampire whilst abroad. After his early death in an accident, neighbours in his village near Belgrade reported seeing him wandering around. When Paole's corpse was exhumed it was found with blood staining its open jaws. The traditional central European test for vampirism was a stake through the heart. To the horror of the witnesses, when this was done to Paole's corpse, copious blood spurted out accompanied by a chilling scream. His corpse was duly burned, as was customary in such cases, and there was some evidence of vampire activity in later years which was blamed on Paole's victims. This illustrates another belief about vampires, that a bite from one condemns the victim also to turn into a vampire.

Vampire accounts proliferated across central Europe in the late 1700s, most of them very similar to the Paole report. Although intellectuals were increasingly sceptical, the belief was very strong in rural areas. Many respected members of communities claimed to have seen evidence of vampires in graves. The French writer Jean-Jacques Rousseau referred, in a letter of 1763, to the mass of witnesses, including "Surgeons, Priests and Magistrates," who were convinced that they had witnessed proof of vampires. The creatures also began to appear in literature; in 1797 the German Johann Wolfgang von Goethe published "The Bride of Corinth," a ballad with a strong vampire theme which opened the way for many other writers. In 1819 a famous literary controversy began when an English writer and poet called John Polidori published a story called "The Vampyre; A Tale." Polidori was the personal physician of the poet Byron, and it was during a stay with him at the Villa Diodati on Lake Geneva that the story took shape. A subsequent quarrel between Byron and Polidori meant that authorship of "The Vampyre" was contested and the disagreement never really settled, but the story itself was widely read and commented on.

By the beginning of the 19th century the details of European vampire belief were broadly agreed. Vampires could be of either sex, though most often male, with characteristically sharp teeth, pale skin and staring eyes. The creatures' activities took

Ψ

RIGHT: The original Dracula, Vlad the Impaler, from a 15th-century likeness.

place at night, and being both magical and dead, vampires were pretty hard to stop – although garlic was generally supposed to act as a deterrent. Becoming a vampire was not thought to be voluntary, nor was it necessarily associated with the Devil or witchcraft. Generally vampires were those who had lived an unpleasant and sinful life, although the innocent could become vampires simply by being victims themselves. Those who had died in irregular circumstances were always suspected; suicides, and those who died excommunicated from the Church or were unavenged murder victims, were likely candidates. The belief was taken so seriously that people who looked a little like the stereotype of the vampire were ostracized; it was thought that they would become vampires after their death. Often they were people who were unusual or different, upon whom suspicion naturally fell.

Getting rid of vampires, as was done with Arnold Paole, was not easy, and could only be done in daytime when the vampire had no power. A hole in the earth over a grave was a sure sign of a vampire occupant. It was said to be used as an exit route at night and could be a means of finishing off the vampire – it was a Romanian custom to pour boiling water down the hole during the day.

Such was the perception of vampires when, at the end of the 19th century, the Irish writer Bram Stoker wrote his historic novel Dracula. The name Dracula was derived from the family of Vlad the Impaler, a 15th-century Romanian ruler whose cruel and bloodthirsty nature earned his father the name of Dracul or Devil, and Vlad the name of Dracula, son of the Devil. Vlad was born in Transylvania, led the life of a tyrant, and made many enemies. He died mysteriously and his body was never identified or buried, but there are no historical suggestions that he was a vampire. The character of Dracula in Stoker's book is the distillation of everything that people have believed about vampires. He has superhuman strength, casts no shadow, can shape-change and can control the elements. He is repelled by garlic, the Sign of the Cross and running water, can enter a house only by invitation and must sleep in his coffin. Having created this creature of unparalleled evil and power, Stoker sets about leading him to his final destruction by the powers of goodness. Dracula was an immediate sensation and spawned many successors. Dealing with the compelling subjects of evil, immortality, and sexual aggression (vampires invariably prey on members of the opposite sex), vampire stories still have the power to fascinate and chill. Even today there are those who believe in the existence of real vampires; there is a Vampire Research Center in New York to which reports of active vampires are made, and vampire societies exist in many European and American cities.

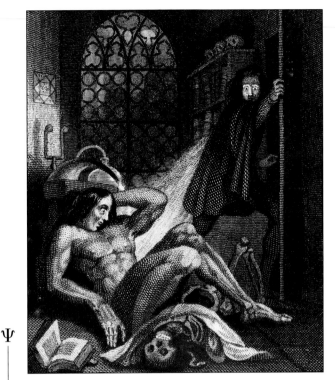

ABOVE: The frontispiece from the original edition of Mary Shelley's Frankenstein, showing how much our image of the character has been shaped by later Hollywood versions.

ABOVE: The Hammer Films Frankenstein, played by Christopher Lee. Truly a monster of man's own making.

NEW DILEMMAS, NEW MONSTERS

The various classes of monsters express our concerns in many areas, among them the definition of our own society, our relationship with the animal world, and the resolution of the undesirable elements in our own natures. As new problems surface, monsters are there to help us confront them. For instance, science now allows us to contemplate radical genetic intervention; new ethical dilemmas surround these developments, and the public is uneasy about the future. Mary Shelley's story *Frankenstein,* written in 1816, told of a man-made monster, the perfect expression of the dangers of society's failure to control science. During the 1990s both the book and a new film interpretation have achieved a fame and popularity undreamed of by their author, as governments grapple with legislation to control genetic experiments.

The dilemmas thrown up by the geneticists' success appear again with Michael Crichton's story *Jurassic Park*, made into a hugely successful feature film in 1992. Dinosaurs have been favorite monsters for many years – implausibly huge, mysterious, with dragon-like characteristics, they had been tamed into a comfortable child's mythology until *Jurassic Park* suggested the possibility of their resurrection. It irresistibly combined archetypal, once-real creatures with contemporary unease about controlling the direction of scientific progress – and monsters, red in tooth and claw, captured the attention of the Western world.

CHAPTER VII

SEEING THE FUTURE

There is something irresistible about taking a look into the future. Most of us agree how intriguing (and how useful) it would be to be able to see ahead, and few people refuse to have their fortune told. Personal columns list palm-readers, astrologers feature in the Yellow Pages of telephone directories, and psychic fairs, featuring a variety of fortune tellers, are promoted as weekend activities. Mass circulation newspapers and magazines could not afford to be without their horoscope columns; despite their brief and general nature, they are a magnet for readers and create a loyal following.

ABOVE: An early 16th-century Eastern astrologer gazes towards the heavens.

ABOVE: A palm-reader's office in New York, a commonplace sight in the city.

RIGHT: The sign for Sagittarius. The zodiac is one of the most ancient systems used by astrologers in their predictions.

A CENTURIES-OLD NEED

If the mention of prophesy, astrology, and soothsaying conjure up images of medieval bearded gentleman in cloaks, consider the role which astrology has been said to play in the decision-making of a recent President of the United States. Kitty Kelly's biography of Nancy Reagan revealed the extent to which the actions of a world leader were determined by the stars. The astrologer Joan Quigley came to know the Reagans in California in the early 1970s, when she first read their horoscopes. As Ronald Reagan's presidency continued, her involvement increased. She made minutely detailed predictions of propitious dates and times, around which the President's itinerary was then constructed. She also read the horoscopes of other world leaders and advised the President about the likelihood of their meetings succeeding. The timing of every journey, every speech and announcement, as well as the predicted outcome of various policy decisions, all came within Quigley's remit, and the White House staff were obliged to plan around her information. After Reagan's retirement she claimed to have

ABOVE: **Ancient**
Chinese divination.

been responsible for all the successes of his term of office, as well as protecting him from threatened disasters.

Paralleling the vogue for personal prediction is our continuing fascination with the prophesies of the past; newspapers often announce the "fulfillment" of yet another of the seer Nostradamus's predictions, reporting that this 16th-century doctor foresaw the details of today's media stars' private lives. Each revelation gains our attention; even sceptics examine the latest claims. Few of us are prepared to give up the idea that a little advance knowledge may be a possibility.

There are logical difficulties, of course. If you see the future and then do something to alter it, it clearly wasn't really the future you saw in the first place. And it takes a fairly firm rejection of our experience of time to believe that somehow we can get ahead of it. Believing that you can foretell the future usually presupposes that some of it, at least, can be changed. If the precognition refers to specific events, then an individual can take steps to avoid them, if necessary, without actually preventing the event. An airline is unlikely to cancel a flight on the basis of someone's premonition of disaster – but that person may avoid the disaster personally by choosing not to fly on that day. Knowing something about the future is obviously valuable, and people feel this most keenly when times are confused and decision-making difficult.

Despite the complexities of seeing into the future, there has never been a shortage of people willing to try. As the Roman philosopher Cicero pointed out in the 1st century BC, "there is not to be found anywhere a race of men, no matter how highly civilized and cultured, or, for that matter, how utterly savage and brutish, which is not firmly convinced that there are portents that point to coming events, and that certain persons are able to recognize these portents and to predict from them what the future holds in store."

Cicero put this talent down to a combination of careful observation and generations of experience, considering it a case of skilled "farsightedness" rather than supernatural power. In this he was rare; in most of the ancient world divination was thought to be more closely linked to the supernatural; the Bible, in Deuteronomy 18: 10-12, put diviners into the same dangerous category as sorcerers and wizards. It was thought presumptuous to try to look at a future decreed by God (unless God had deliberately revealed it); and later, in the 15th century, Dante described in his *Inferno* fortune-tellers in Hell with their heads twisted around, capable only of seeing behind them. Yet outside the Judeo-Christian cultures diviners and prophets were (and are) regarded as straightforward practitioners providing a service.

Ancient societies believed that life was full of references to the future – omens were everywhere, waiting to throw light on what lay in store. In the Middle East the

Babylonians, the Assyrians, and the Sumerians were constantly looking at the skies, the behavior of animals, and the elements for clues. Each of these was significant; eclipses, earthquakes, volcanoes and storms were particularly potent signs. For obvious reasons societies tended to concentrate on the natural features that were most evident. Country-dwellers would pay special attention to the mood and movements of animals and birds, the inhabitants of Italy relied on volcanic phenomena and atmospheric disturbances, while the Egyptians, faced with endless flat plains, looked to the stars. Everyone knew roughly what the signs meant but certain members of each society were specially skilled in interpreting the omens and giving advice based upon them.

The art of all divination lies in the interpretation of seemingly unrelated patterns to reveal a predetermined destiny. All systems are based on associations between shapes, images, events, and numbers which the skilled interpreter can "read". *A Compendium of Divinations*, a 17th-century survey by John Gaule, listed the types of divination that had been recorded. They included, among the more usual methods of divining by air, numbers, palms of hands, birds, casting lots and dreams, more esoteric varieties such as gastromancy (divining by the sounds of the stomach), tyromancy (by the coagulation of cheese), and sycomancy (by figs).

In many societies divination is a formalized way of finding out what the following days will bring. Where this is routine, predictions are sought in much the same way as we in modern Western society would check a weather forecast – it is a matter-of-fact method of planning more efficiently. When predictions go wrong the reaction is the same as ours – the forecasters got it wrong. We feel that our weather forecast is based on valid scientific principles, which make sense to us; the forecast is often wrong, but this does not shake our belief in it. In other societies, divination is believed to be on an equally firm footing, and just as liable to be affected by the interpreters' shortcomings.

ORACLES

Oracles are a widespread means of divination; in some cases the role of the interpreter can be crucial. The most interesting characteristic of oracles is that they permit messages to pass between the human and the divine. Given that there is an all-powerful deity or power controlling events and mapping out the future, it should be possible to share some of this knowledge by simply asking. The messages may be simple, as in the case of the Azande oracle (see page 145), or as complex as those of the most famous oracle of all, the Pythia of Delphi on the slopes of Mount Parnassus in Greece.

In the 4th, 5th, and 6th centuries BC the god Apollo was the centre of a popular cult, and Greeks flocked to Delphi to consult the Oracle, paying about two days' wages for each question. The sacred site of the Oracle was one of the few places where the gods could be contacted, consulted, and induced to give a response. The messages were channeled through a medium who had to be detached from the usual human condition, usually in a trance state. Training improved the ability of the medium to enter the trance and deliver the responses; mediums were considered to

be outside the process – mere mouthpieces, who may have had no understanding and little memory of what they had said. The messages were invariably convoluted, and needed decoding by trained priests. Interpretation was skilled; the responses were sufficiently ambiguous for the Oracle never to be seen as completely wrong. During the 6th century BC King Croesus was anxious to know what would happen if he declared war on the Persians. The Oracle's reply was that a great empire would be destroyed. Croesus took this to refer to the Persians, and, reassured, went to battle. Unfortunately for him, it was his own great army which was destroyed.

The Oracle's pronouncements were usually diplomatically couched to avoid causing offence, and were often deliberately obscure so that only those the message was intended for would understand. Many hours were spent puzzling over the cryptic responses, neatly delivered in hexameter verse. Certainly its customers were happy with the service, which continued for more than 1,000 years.

Part of the Oracle's success may have been due to its very centrality and popularity. The priests were in constant contact with people from all over the empire, from farmers to soldiers and political leaders, and the Greek city-states regularly sent officials to consult the Oracle on all important matters. So Delphi was full of travellers, bringing all the latest news, and the priests' facility for intelli-

ABOVE TOP: The site of the Delphic Oracle in Greece, the Classical era's most prestigious centre of divination.

gence-gathering was unsurpassed. With their fingers so firmly on the pulse, and given the convenient tradition of elliptical pronouncements, they were therefore able to maintain a high success rate.

There is evidence also that people often consult an oracle for reassurance and confirmation of something they intend to do anyway, and so will always interpret what it says in that light – undoubtedly the case with King Croesus. Divination strengthens the resolve of those whose mind is almost made up and forces the indecisive to take a stand. Oracle priests, like all other fortune-tellers, combine whatever supernatural assistance they may receive with efficient information gathering and good psychology.

ABOVE: Consulting the Oracle, as depicted on a Greek vase of the 5th century BC.

Gradually the Greeks, influenced by their philosophers Plato. Aristotle, and Pythagoras, moved away from the Oracle toward astrology as a means of prediction. Tibet, however, retained the state oracles which traditionally assisted their leaders. One of these oracles warned the present Dalai Lama of the Chinese invasion in 1959 and enabled him to leave Lhasa in time. He has an oracle in exile at Dharamsala in India, which he consults on a regular basis.

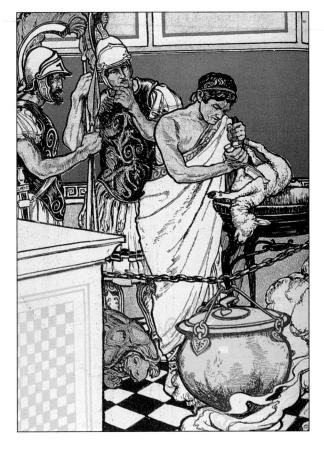

ABOVE: King Croesus tested the Oracle before trusting its advice. It passed by correctly divining that on a certain day he boiled a lamb and a tortoise in a brass cauldron.

ABOVE: The Dalai Lama, who still maintains an oracle in exile.

Oracles need not be ambiguous: many of the simpler sort deliver straight "yes" or "no" answers. Some do not even require a specialist medium or place. Casting lots (cleromancy) is a means by which a specific question can be answered, and takes many forms. A popular method in classical times required a pot of coloured beans and a strip of lead. A question could be written on the lead strip, which was then inserted into the pot. If it came out with a bean of one colour clinging to it the answer to the question would be yes; if the bean was another colour, the answer would be no.

Oracles such as this are known all over the world and are still in common use. In the southern Sudan, members of the Azande people would not think of making a journey or planting crops without consulting an oracle, of which there is a full range to suit different needs. A straightforward question, such as whether today would be an auspicious day for planting, could be quickly asked of a rubbing-board – simply two pieces of smoothed wood which are rubbed together. The question is put to the oracle; if one piece of wood catches against the other the answer is yes and if the pieces glide smoothly it is no. This kind of oracle decides minor matters rapidly and weeds out preliminary questions in more serious affairs. Most adult Azande men have a rubbing oracle to consult whenever necessary, but they sometimes find it

ABOVE: A Dogon diviner in Mali, West Africa, skilfully interpreting a ground nut oracle.

unreliable. For matters such as the identity of a witch, serious disputes, adultery, marriages, or major hunting expeditions, they turn to less convenient but more convincing oracles. In all dangerous or socially important matters a specialist diviner will be employed; on behalf of the enquirer he will ask the questions of *benge*, the poison oracle.

The poison oracle takes the form of small amounts of a strychnine-like substance which are fed to a succession of chickens while the problem is being outlined to the oracle. The oracle is asked to decide between two possibilities, such as whether or not a woman is committing adultery, by causing the chicken to die if the answer is positive. If the chicken does die, the oracle may be asked to confirm the identity of the other man by causing the next chicken to die when the right name is put to it. Given enough chickens and enough poison, a man can continue consulting the oracle until all his questions are answered. Important pieces of information are always confirmed by asking the oracle to repeat its answer with another chicken. Any man who is wealthy enough to own chickens and poison can operate and consult the oracle, providing he has observed certain ritual taboos. Women and younger, less prosperous men have to persuade someone else to question the oracle for them. If the oracle is seen to go wildly wrong in its responses, the error is put down to poor attention to the rituals.

Western outsiders immediately conclude that oracle operators cheat by regulating the amount of poison administered to the chickens, or by changing the pressure on the rubbing board, but this seems not to be the case. Naturally matters put to the oracle, and the way in which they are framed, reflect the questioner's concerns and his existing convictions, so that often (but not always) the oracle is satisfactorily confirming what is already believed. Sir Edward Evans-Pritchard, a British social anthropologist who lived with the Azande in the 1920s and wrote the first complete account of their beliefs, found no evidence of conscious manipulation. He considered that, having accepted the belief that the oracles were truthful, the system made perfect sense. Although he did not believe in oracles himself, "I always kept a supply of poison for the use of my household and neighbours and we regulated our affairs in accordance with the oracles' decisions. I may remark that I found this as satisfactory a way of running my home and affairs as any other I know of."

PROPHETS

Oracles allow some communication with the controlling powers, but only of the most impersonal sort. "Prophets" are people who receive a personal divine revelation which gives insight into the wishes of the deity as well as telling them what will happen in the future. Most major religions are founded on the belief that humans are periodically selected to receive guidance and act as a mouthpiece for their particular god. Moses, considered the mightiest of the Bible prophets, (Deuteronomy 34:10-12) was given the Ten Commandments by his God and told how to secure a future for the chosen people. His story, and that of at least 18 other leading prophets, is recorded in the Old Testament and these revelations form the cornerstone of Judeo-Christian beliefs. Prophets sometimes have to accept divine instructions against their will; St Paul, in the New Testament, was compelled by a revelation which changed his life.

Muslims believe that Muhammad was chosen to be the Seal, the last of the many thousands of prophets, receiving from the archangel Gabriel the exact text of the Koran. Dictated over a 20-year period during the 7th century, the Koran was intended to give directions for daily life and prayer. Muhammad entered a trance state in order to receive his revelations, which emphasized the need for him to convert the then pagan Arab people to a purer form of the Judeo-Christian religion. His divine messages avoided the misinterpretations which had distorted Christianity; the Koran gave its followers access to the undiluted word and intention of God. Muhammad then began preaching his revelations, calling his believers Muslims, derived from a word meaning "they who surrender to God." Over the centuries the numbers of Muslims have grown to the 100 million estimated today, and the religion remains rooted in obedience to the Koran and reverence for the prophet Muhammad.

More recently the Church of Jesus Christ of Latter Day Saints, also known as the Mormon Church, a successful modern Christian denomination with more than 4 million members worldwide, was founded by a prophet who claimed divine revelation. Joseph Smith, son of a poor American farming family, had a

BELOW: Moses received personal communications from God, among them the Ten Commandments which form the bedrock of Judeo-Christian morality.

Ψ

Ψ

LEFT: A veiled depiction of Muhammad, believed by Muslims to be the last and greatest of the prophets.

BELOW LEFT: William Miller, who incorrectly prophecied the end of the world.

series of visions in the early 1820s in which God appeared to him and promised to reveal the one true religion. Later, an angel, Moroni, came in a vision and told him where to find gold plates upon which would be written the basis for a new Church of Christ. Smith located the plates, which were inscribed with hieroglyphics and accompanied by seer stones. Each plate was translated by Smith through a visionary process which resulted in *The Book of the Mormon*, published in 1830, the same year in which the Church of Christ, as it was first known, was set up.

Smith's Church members came into heavy conflict with their fellow Americans, not least over their belief in polygamy, and violence marked the early history of the Mormons. After Smith's assassination in 1844 a new leader, Brigham Young, took the Mormons to the freedom of Utah, where in Salt Lake City the revitalized Church began its main period of growth. Conflict with the government over polygamy continued until the Mormons abandoned their policy in 1890.

Other modern prophets have been less concerned with making a better world than with predicting the end of the present one. On numerous occasions dates have been selected and believers have made detailed preparations, only to find the world rolling on much as usual. William Miller, a New England preacher, predicted that the world would end on three different occasions during 1843-4. He gained support when traditional omens such as comets and meteors appeared, and thousands of believers proved willing to sell their property and gather on hillsides to await the final moments. When the third prediction failed, Miller's followers seemed to abandon their commitment to the end of the world; the group became unfocused and began to break into a number of smaller sects. One of these groups became even more successful than the original; the Seventh-Day Adventist Church now numbers more than 3 million.

PREMONITION AND PRECOGNITION

The words of the major prophets may have influenced millions of lives, but for most of us, any glimpses into the future we may achieve will be without divine assistance. Premonition, a common form of foreknowledge, is a less clear and detailed prediction of the future, more a feeling than a vision. Usually it is a sense of anxiety or dread, a knowing that something is going to go wrong.

More detailed premonitions do sometimes occur. One of the most tragic cases concerned the events at Aberfan in Wales in 1966. Huge mountains of coal waste traditionally surround mining villages; on this occasion one became unstable and slid down over part of the village, killing more than 140 children and teachers in their school. Two days previously a local child, Eryl Mai Jones, had told her mother that she expected to die soon, but was unworried by the prospect. Later she said that she had looked at the school and seen it covered in "black stuff." She died in the accident. Hundreds of miles away a woman had a dream of children in a building, in great distress. Her feeling of dread would not abate when she awoke, and she was so convinced of an impending disaster that she telephoned her daughter-in-law to tell her to safeguard her small children although, according to the daughter-in-law who received the call, "she thought it was more likely to have been a school, because it was a lot of children all together in a long room." The Aberfan slag-heaps collapsed just half an hour after the call. Three subsequent surveys uncovered evidence of more than 200 premonitions, many quite specific to the disaster, during the weeks before the accident.

Evaluation of premonitions and precognition is tricky because we only pay attention to them after a disaster has occurred. It is not known how many people have these experiences without anything coming of them, how many missed flights arrive safely at their destination. The timescale is important, too; if you dream of an earthquake, sooner or later there will be one. An interesting survey was carried out in the 1970s by researcher W. J. Cox, who discovered that trains involved in rail accidents carried fewer passengers (sometimes dramatically so) on the accident day than on the same day in previous weeks. There is no obvious reason for this, and it is tempting to conclude that premonitions, perhaps unconscious, had influenced potential travellers.

The English playwright and novelist J. B. Priestley took a particular interest in precognition and recorded numerous cases. One well-documented example concerned a British Navy officer who was sailing in convoy off the coast of Scotland in 1916. He was standing on the bridge when he had a strong, vision-like premonition of a man in the water. As the ship approached the offshore island that the officer had seen in his vision, he ordered a boat to be made ready. To his surprise and embarrassment they sailed uneventfully past the island. As other members of the convoy drew level with the island, however, there were sudden shouts of "man overboard" from two of the other ships. The prepared lifeboat was instantly launched and rescued both men. Priestley believed that such incidents can only be explained by hypothesizing the existence of further dimensions which occasionally intersect to give glimpses of the future. People may not always be aware of the overlap, or realize that they are envisioning the future. Such an explanation might explain the extraordinary

ABOVE: The Old Testament story of Joseph predicting the future by interpreting the dreams of the Pharaoh.

LEFT: The sinking of the ill-fated liner Titanic, accurately foreshadowed in a novel published 14 years earlier.

similarities between a fictional account of the sinking of the *SS Titan* and the actual sinking of the *Titanic,* which took place 14 years later in 1912. Morgan Robertson's *The Wreck of the Titan* parallels the real-life disaster with disturbing accuracy, matching the details more closely than coincidence could explain.

The experience of precognition is most likely to occur in dreams. These unsettling glimpses into the future are usually unsolicited; they simply happen to people without any effort on their part. Sometimes people who have had prophetic dreams become more tuned to these possibilities and go on to develop their psychic capacities further, but the sheer number of people who have experienced some form of precognition suggests that many of us are more sensitive to psychic phenomena than we think.

Dreaming the future dates from earliest times, and has always been the most acceptable means of precognition. In the Old Testament of the Bible Joseph rises to power through his ability, not only to have precognitive dreams himself, but to explain the dreams of others. His successful interpretation of the Pharaoh's dreams resulted in Egypt surviving the seven years of famine which the dreams foretold;

150

Joseph himself reached a powerful position within the Pharaoh's government, an outcome which his own dreams had predicted. Such a broad prophesy involves the problem of changing the future; the predicted years of famine duly occurred, but foreknowledge of them meant that their consequences could be reduced. Prophesy through dreams was approved in the Old Testament, even when other sorts of divination were suspect, and dream interpretation could be a powerful political weapon, legitimizing the course of action which a ruler intended to follow.

Sometimes prophetic dreams need no interpretation, and are detailed and easily verified. In 1946, for instance, Lord Kilbracken dreamed the names of a succession of horse race winners. Each time, he dreamed that he was reading a newspaper reporting the race after the event. All his predictions were correct, even when, the following year, his dreams changed to images of the colors worn by the winners. Unfortunately, this useful ability began to fade and finally left him altogether.

Many dreams prophecying death are also fairly unambiguous. The night before his assassination the Roman Emperor Caligula dreamed that the god Jupiter had kicked him out of the heavens, sending him plummeting through space. Even more clear-cut was the dream of Abraham Lincoln, President of the United States, who in 1865 awoke one morning in the White House to report a dream in which he saw his own body lying in state, surrounded by weeping bystanders who described how the President had been assassinated. This awful portent became fact less than a month later, when Lincoln was shot dead during a visit to the theatre. The dream need not, however, be experienced by the actual victim; in 1812 a mining engineer, John Williams, had a detailed dream in which Spencer Perceval, Prime Minister of Britain, was shot in the lobby of the House of Commons. Williams described his dream to family and friends, but could not decide whether to warn Perceval personally. Eight days after the dream, Perceval was assassinated in exactly the same circumstances.

LEFT: President Abraham Lincoln had precognition of his death in a dream, but he had not predicted the details of his assassination.

OPPOSITE: The signs of Taurus and Gemini, depicted above the appropriate season. This 15th-century painting is one of the earliest to link everyday human life with the movement of the stars.

Ψ

BELOW: An Egyptian astronomer and mathematician of the 2nd century, whose work built upon a tradition already 3,000 years old.

Premonition and precognition give tantalizing and sometimes frightening glimpses of the future, but their occurrence is so capricious that they cannot form a reliable guide. Ancient systems of divination provided useful ways to answer questions, but were intellectually unsatisfying. Astrology filled the gap, offering the most complete system of predicting the future at the same time as understanding the present. It began its development when humans first looked at the night sky and noticed that it was always changing. The earliest naming and tracking of the stars took place 5,000 years ago in Mesopotamia (modern Iraq) this knowledge spread to the Egyptians, who incorporated astrology into their religion, and to the Greeks, who refined and extended its use as a science. A Babylonian sect called the Chaldeans built ziggurats (stepped pyramid-like towers) in order to observe the skies, and by about 3000 BC had developed the notion that there was a connection between the movement of heavenly bodies and the outcome of human lives.

Astrology was first used to predict major events – wars, bad harvests or rebellions. Practitioners looked to the skies for unusual movements, such as meteors or shooting stars, which were linked to terrestrial events. In addition, the stars were used to provide guidance for the auspicious timing of important actions. Around 500 BC the Chaldeans began to speculate that the stage of the astral cycle at which a person is born could influence their character and their destiny; they were moving in the direction of personal horoscopes. The 12 constellations were named after animals, and became the signs of the zodiac. It was the Greeks who developed and elaborated the casting of personal horoscopes into the method we still employ, although the names we use are the Roman ones. Less than 200 years before Christ, the innovative astronomer and mathematician Ptolemy wrote the *Tetrabiblios*, a comprehensive manual including all that was currently known about the stars and their movements, as well as full instructions for casting horoscopes; it is still in use today. The Greeks and Romans were reluctant to take decisions without consulting the stars, and felt that planetary influence was crucial. A spectacular use of astrology was the tracking down of the infant Jesus by the Magi, who were astrologers, probably Persian, who had read a messianic prophesy in the stars. Zoroaster, the Persian prophet, had predicted a messiah in the 6th century BC, and it was the astral pattern foreseen by him which had sent the Magi to Bethlehem. Ironically, early Christians disapproved of astrology; they felt that it implied that fate was predestined and went counter to their gospel of redemption. The Christian Emperor Constantine denounced it in 333 AD, and astrology became unacceptable in Europe for several hundred years.

Meanwhile, Arab astrologers continued to practice their art, and while astrology waned in Europe between the 4th and 12th centuries it flourished in China, India, Tibet, and even Central America. By the early Middle Ages Europe was welcoming astrology back from the Arabs as part of the new

Ψ  Ψ

Ψ ABOVE: Twelve Arabic zodiac signs, based on planetary images.

RIGHT: William Lilly, a 17th-century London astrologer who had more business than he could handle.

interest in science, alchemy, philosophy, and medicine; it had been re-introduced by Spanish Jews who had studied it as part of their interest in the mystical system of the Hebrew Cabbala. In the medieval world-view it was interconnected with other disciplines. It was taught in universities and regarded as essential, for instance, in medical training; each part of the body had links with the zodiac, as did chemical elements and herbs which were used in treatment, and doctors had to be able to incorporate all this knowledge into their work.

As the modern, rationalist view of science began to form in the 17th century astrology found itself again not quite respectable and was quietly dropped from university syllabuses. It could not conform to the new demands for proof, and was no longer accepted as a science. Its use as propaganda by the opposing sides in the Thirty Years War (1618-1648) in Europe hastened its fall from grace – the most learned exponents were apparently predicting directly conflicting outcomes. The decline of astrology in intellectual circles was not immediately followed in the mass of the population. The surviving casebooks of several 17th-century London astrologers, including William Lilly, who predicted the London Plague and Great Fire of London in 1665 and 1666, show that practitioners were run off their feet, handling up to 2,000 private cases a year as well as formulating their general predictions. Clients ranged from the mighty inquiring about affairs of state (Charles II consulted the astrologer Ashmole in 1673 about his future relationship with Parliament) to the humble (Lilly was asked in 1659 to foretell whether a man arrested for stealing would be hanged). While the astrologers were busy, the astrological almanacs which had begun to appear were selling briskly. But despite this popular appeal the development of the art had been interrupted, and there were few important practitioners in the succeeding centuries.

The appeal of astrology as a personal predicter survived all adversities, however, and now, if anything, is gaining in strength. Today there are two types: "pop" astrology, where daily, weekly, or monthly predictions are published for each star sign, and the casting of individual horoscopes. The popular press "stars" are usually vague enough to cover most eventualities and offer entertainment value as much as anything. By contrast privately drawn horoscopes are based on the precise time of birth and go into considerable detail. Today's astrologers use data from recent astronomical researches, frequently processed by computer, to build up complex charts. They are often uncannily accurate and those who regularly consult astrologers are convinced of their value.

A startlingly successful fortune-teller of recent years made use of palm reading and crystal gazing as well as astrology; she had prophetic visions about the future of her subjects. Born in California in 1918, Jeane Dixon had heightened psychic gifts even as a child. She had some spontaneous visions, but her main prophecies came from her crystal ball. Among her successful predictions were: the sudden deaths of Carole Lombard, Dag Hammarskjold, Marilyn Monroe, John F. Kennedy, Robert Kennedy, Martin Luther King, and the three young American astronauts killed in the Apollo rocket fire in 1967. Her visions of individuals' fates were generally more accurate than her political prophesies; although she predicted the date of the partition of India and the political defeat of Churchill after World War II, many of her other war predictions failed.

CRYSTAL GAZING

For most of us, "crystal-gazing" summons images of the fortune-telling gypsy hunched over her crystal ball. But for many centuries the power to see visions in reflections has been the gift of those who look into the future. "Scrying" is the name given to all forms of this activity. Any reflective surface will do, from a polished thumbnail (used in Arab countries) through polished metals, water (either in a lake or in a bowl), glass, ink and, indeed, a polished crystal. Scryers seem able to improve their skills with practise. By concentrating on the reflecting surface and emptying the mind, almost anyone can eventually see patterns and images. Those with clairvoyant abilities can see clear pictures of places and people and even hear conversations. The crystal or other surface becomes the focus and prompter of a trance-like state in which predictions can occur. As with much oracular divination, the images may need interpretation before they become comprehensible. Patterns which mean

BELOW: Scrying, or crystal gazing, has been a divinatory method for centuries. A simple technique enables images to be visualized on any polished surface.

Ψ

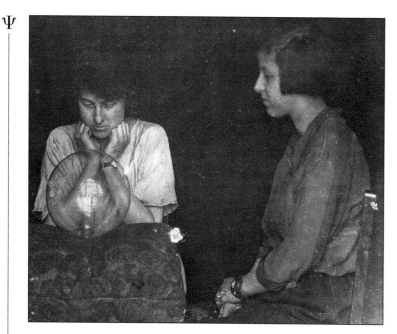

nothing to the layman resolve into a language for the skilled practitioner.

Scrying was a standard procedure in European divination until after the end of the Middle Ages. John Dee, the court magician and astrologer to Elizabeth I, was well known for *not* being able to scry. He had a polished crystal, but although he was deeply involved with magic and alchemy and could make accurate astrological predictions he was unable to see into the crystal. He was forced to employ scryers to do it for him, and thus entered into a long partnership with Edward Kelley, who appeared to have an undeniable gift. Kelley's scrying revealed, among other things, the Enochian language, through which angels communicated with Kelley and Dee. Many mysteries surround John Dee; he was a scholarly and intelligent man, yet may have been taken in by Kelley, whom many considered to be fraudulent. There are suggestions that Dee was a spy for Elizabeth, as well as an astrologer, and that Enochian (a perfectly consistent, functioning language) was used as code. Elizabeth refers to him as her "ubiquitous eyes", and Dee signed letters to her with a pair of eyes followed by a seven – 007. Although Dee never did master scrying, he managed to foresee the telescope and its military use, to predict Mary Queen of Scots' execution, along with its date in 1587, and not only to foresee the Armada in 1588 but to tell Elizabeth about the way in which it would be defeated.

Ψ

NOSTRADAMUS

John Dee was a typical 16th-century intellectual, dabbling in astrology, medicine, and prophesy, but his achievements are not widely known. Nostradamus's name, in contrast, is known to millions. Long term prophesies exercise a particular fascination; their appeal, especially when backed up by early success, is undeniable. Even so, the impact of Nostradamus is extraordinary. His major work, *Propheties*, first published in its complete form in 1568, has been in print ever since. During these four centuries every word of the hundreds of quatrains that he wrote has been analyzed, pondered, and variously interpreted. This is not a straightforward task, as the quatrains, written in medieval Provencal French with smatterings of Latin and Greek, are metaphorical and often deliberately obscure. The prophesies are not arranged in chronological order and, even when translated, appear on first reading to make very little sense. Yet Nostradamus's prophesies are, if anything, growing in popularity; they are the subject of dozens of books, articles, and films, and even feature in advertisements. The interpretation of the quatrains is hotly contested among scholars who have spent their professional life deciphering the texts.

Who was this man whose influence has lasted so dramatically for centuries after his death? Michel de Nostradame was born in St Rémy de Provence, France, in December 1503, into an intellectual family who had converted from Judaism to Catholicism. He was an intelligent, literary child, who went on to medicine at the University of Montpellier. Medical science in those days relied heavily on astrology and philosophy, in both of which Nostradamus had always had an interest. He possessed a reputation for unconventional thinking, which he applied to the most pressing medical problem of the time, the plague. Sixteenth-century doctors were faced with a devastating disease whose origins and spread they did not understand. They knew of no treatment which could help, and Nostradamus realized that much of what they did actually made things worse. He abandoned the practise of bleeding his patients, advising instead fresh air, and, if possible, fresh running water. He believed that medicines could cure, and devoted much time to developing new ones. He became both successful and popular, until his wife and all his children caught the plague and died. After this he spent several years travelling around France and Italy, collecting medicines and extending his pharmacological knowledge.

BELOW: Nostradamus, author of famous and enduring prophesies.

MICHEL NOSTRADAMUS.
Medecin,
Né à S.ᵗRemy, en Provence, le 14 Décemb. 1503.
Mort le 2, juillet 1566.

At last he settled down in Salon, Provence, remarried – and began to prophecy the future. It is unclear how exactly he went about it. Astrology undoubtedly figured in the process; he was also a scryer, using a bowl of water to concentrate his visions. Although he made careful astrological calculations, he felt that the events themselves came to him as prophetic visions. These visions he recorded in quatrains, four-line verses which he grouped by the hundred and called centuries. The first of the centuries were published in 1555, and their fame soon spread. In 1557, as the educated classes puzzled over the verses, Nostradamus was summoned to see the Queen of France, Catherine de Médicis, who was anxious to know the future fate of her family. Nostradamus had a gift for clairvoyance – certainly Catherine was satisfied with the horoscopes he provided, and remained so. One of his most famous predictions seemed to tell, in an early quatrain, of the death of Henri II, her husband, in a duel. This subsequently came about, and although not all the details of the quatrain were verified, those who had heard it were awestruck.

This impressive success made Nostradamus's reputation secure, but also made him more interesting to the Inquisitors, the officials of the Roman Catholic Church, whose job it was to investigate anyone who might be dabbling in magical,

Ψ RIGHT: Catherine de Médicis, with her sons Charles IX and Henri III. Catherine employed Nostradamus to cast horoscopes for her family.

Ψ

158

possibly diabolical arts. The Inquisitors were vigilant in their crusade against heresy and witchcraft predicting the future would have immediately put Nostradamus under suspicion of dealing with the Devil. So Nostradamus was careful to extol the virtues of the Church and observe its practise to the letter, while publicly denouncing magic and sorcery. Fortunately he also had the protection of the Queen and knew when to keep a low profile. He even burned his own library, declaring that the ancient magical texts were dangerous and should be destroyed. By these means he managed to live safely and comfortably until his health began to fail in 1566, and seven years after the prophecied death of Henri II he died at Salon, aged 62. The centuries were published in full after his death, and have absorbed interpreters ever since.

There is little real certainty about the scale of Nostradamus's success as a prophet. The quatrains are essentially ambiguous, and much of their meaning must be guessed. Scholars, through careful translation, have found that Nostradamus had several slightly baffling habits; he often abbreviated names, or used historical or classical allusions instead, and some key words are given in the form of anagrams or disguised in other ways. Nostradamus felt reluctant to spell out his predictions too baldly. He considered that the world, and particularly its leaders, would be unable to cope with the unvarnished truth. He feared for himself, as well; he was nervous of the Inquisition and of offending powerful people. "But now I am willing for the general good to enlarge myself in dark and abstruse sentences, so that my predictions will not wholly offend present sensibilities. The whole work is therefore written in a nebulous rather than a plainly prophetic form . . ."

By admitting to deliberately disguising his meanings, Nostradamus gave *carte blanche* to the numerous decoders who have seized upon his work ever since. Scholars have been able to work out the recurrent symbolism and to identify certain tricks about names, and these have allowed some sense to be made of many of the quatrains. But this has not been enough for some recent commentators, who have gone further and, by substituting certain letters and creating anagrams, claim to have discovered secret codes which can unlock the quatrains. With these methods highly detailed and specific predictions have been extracted, but such tortuous translations seem to be the least successful or convincing of the interpretations; and many have already failed. Take quatrain III. 65: *"When the tomb of the great Roman is found, after a day a Pope will be elected. He will not be approved by the Senate, his blood poisonous in the sacred chalice."* This is one of several possible translations from the original. Many meanings have been teased from this, among them that the Prince and Princess of Wales would become King and Queen of England on 2 May, 1992, an event which most definitely did not take place.

Even taking the translations which seem to convey Nostradamus's original meaning sensibly, many of the verses are open to a number of interpretations. Any contemporary event can find an echo somewhere among nearly 1,000 quatrains; there are plenty of commentators who have done just that, making ingenious but dubious connections between 20th-century events and this 16th-century best-seller.

Those who try to wring detailed relevance and meaning from the quatrains are perhaps missing the point; the enduring value of Nostradamus is that he has provided us with a long-lived oracle. His prophesies carry enough ambiguity to be applied across time and space, while embodying the vital events which preoccupy every generation – scandal, war, famine, disease, and revolution. Whatever our concerns, we can search the quatrains and Nostradamus will supply an answer – or at least a focus for our anxieties and a framework for decision-making. And like any other oracle, if it turns out to be wrong there is always an explanation – an error of interpretation or timescale, perhaps. There is plenty of time for them all to come true, one way or another. Like other oracles, Nostradamus will yield whatever his questionners need to see. William Fulke, a 16th-century sceptic, declared Nostradamus's works to be "in such dark wrinkles of obscurity that no man would pick out of them either sense or understanding. Without doubt, he has heard of the oracles of Apollo . . . which were obscure, double and such as might chance both ways. . ."

Most responses to oracles and prophesies are formulated on an unconscious level, but sometimes they are deliberately manipulated. During World War II the Nazis became aware of a young Swiss astrologer and Nostradamus interpreter called Ernst Krafft. Goebbels, the propaganda minister, saw the potential for spreading a Nostradamus prediction which pointed to a German victory. Krafft was employed to come up with suitable interpretations from the *Propheties*. As British intelligence became aware of Goebbels' activities they resorted to similar methods. Their most painstaking achievement was a faked edition of 50 Nostradamus quatrains which pointed to Hitler's defeat and death.

PALMISTRY

Nostradamus specialized in predicting the lives of politically relevant figures and large-scale world events. But many of us are more curious about our personal futures. For centuries people have believed that each person's destiny is recorded in the lines of the palm of the hand. Palmistry, once known as chiromancy, was practiced in India and China at least 1,000 years before Christ. The Greeks, including Aristotle and Pliny, considered it a valid science. Based on detailed reading of the lines and configuration of the palm of the hand, palmistry provides not only an indication of character but a prediction of future fortune in areas such as romance, business, and health. It was too close to heresy and witchcraft for the Middle Ages, and the Church banned it. Needless to say it continued, in a very low key, until it became popular again at the end of the 19th century.

The best-known of the turn-of-the-century palmists was Cheiro, born in Ireland as William John Warner in 1866. Unlike many of those who predict the future, Cheiro was not afraid to be specific. He gave not only events, but dates; amazingly, they turned out to be accurate. Among those impressed with his success were Oscar Wilde, King Edward VII of England, King Leopold II of the Belgians, the Tsar of Russia, the Russian monk Rasputin, and the British general Lord Kitchener. When put to the test by a New York newspaper Cheiro scored a series of direct hits with anonymous palm prints. The way he predicted major events was by stating their effects on his clients; for instance, he warned the editor W. T. Stead not to travel by water during April 1912. Stead ignored this advice and died in the sinking of the

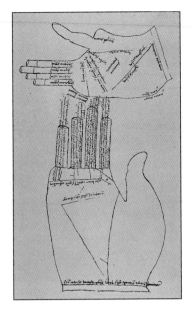

Ψ Titanic. Despite his unprecedented success in foreseeing the affairs of others, Cheiro allowed himself to become involved in a business venture which ended in failure. Although bankrupt, he recovered and went on to finish his days in Hollywood, still successfully reading the palms of the rich and famous.

ABOVE: Caravaggio's *Fortune Teller* is careful to observe every detail of her client - as well as his hand - as she makes her reading. Ψ

ABOVE LEFT: A medieval guide to palmistry, showing important lines and their interpretation.

THE TAROT

So much do we accept the naturalness of fortune-telling today that no one would be surprised at any house containing a set of Tarot cards. The earliest known Tarot decks date from the 15th century, but the pack did not achieve its present form until well into the 18th century; the most popular current images date only from 1910, when A. E.Waite, a member of the Hermetic Order of the Golden Dawn (an influential magical order which included the Irish poet W. B.Yeats among its members), designed a pack based on his own brand of magical symbolism. They are similar to modern playing cards (which can also be used for divination), but are divided into the Major Arcana of 22 cards and the Minor Arcana of 56 cards. Each card is illustrated with a symbol, and the skill of reading the cards lies in the interpretation of each symbol, not just on its own, but modified by the other cards lying in proximity to it. Many different Tarot decks are available, each one richly and powerfully illustrated in its own distinctive style. It is easy to see why the cards have exercised such a fascination; their compelling imagery hints at the mysteries of fate, destiny, and revelation.

The Tarot deck is first shuffled and then the cards are laid out in various arrangements or "spreads" after which the pattern is read. The reading is based on a knowledge of the meaning of the cards and their positions, but, as with all forms of divination, some people get better results than others. For more than a simple reading, an intuitive gift is required. Marie-Anne-Adelaide Lenormand, born in France in 1772, was one of the most accomplished Tarot readers. She appears to have had

WHEEL of FORTUNE

JUSTICE .

Ψ

ABOVE: Mademoiselle
Lenormand, famous
for her skill in reading
the Tarot.

ABOVE RIGHT: The
Tarot deck of 1910,
designed for A. E.
Waite.

various clairvoyant gifts, but her skills with the cards led to her becoming consultant
to the Empress Josephine. The leading figures in Revolutionary Paris came for read-
ings in which she accurately forecast marriages, births, journeys, ruin, and death.
She became very wealthy but was generous to those in need, which may account for
the huge turn-out at her funeral in 1843. She had in fact died sooner than she predicted. She spoke often of the dire significance of a raven's visit, and suffered a stroke
after apparently seeing one fly into her bedroom; in fact the bird was an innocent
pigeon, misidentified by her failing sight.

SEEKING THE FUTURE IN THE COMPUTER AGE

The few flashes of precognition that some of us experience, together with the success
of fortune-tellers such as Jeane Dixon, keep open the possibility that time is indeed
another dimension, the laws of which we do not understand. Our human tendency
is to want to believe that the future can be known.

Most people who approach an oracle or a fortune-teller want to know the future
in order to deal with the present. Decisions become easier to make the more information we have. The Chinese *I Ching* or *Book of Changes* positively urges us to contemplate our problems and our attitude to them. Developed around 2852 BC by the
Emperor Fu-hsi, the *I Ching* has been in use in China for 4,000 years. After throwing
a die (or tossing yarrow stalks in the traditional method) six times, the petitioner
uses a simple code to translate the die numbers into hexagrams, patterns of continu-
ous and broken lines which can be interpreted in the light of the stated problem to
show the probable outcomes of different courses of action. Standard interpretations
are available for each hexagram, although these produce cruder evaluations than a
skilled interpreter. The *I Ching* does not give precise directions, merely advice which
petitioners must consider and analyze for themselves. The system is based on the
ancient principle of duality, the opposition between yin and yang which creates and

channels energy. Attention to the ritual of the divination and finely tuned interpretation make it infinitely adaptable; it can be used for domestic and personal decisions as well as affairs of state. Translated into English only this century, the *I Ching* has grown rapidly in popularity in Europe and America, prompted by the huge success of Japanese businessmen who claimed to base all their decisions on its guidance. There is even a computer software version designed to help with business decisions. Hexagrams can be interpreted under specialist categories, such as "investment" or "marketing".

There has never been a blind belief in seers or their prophesies. Prophesy has played its part throughout human history, but not just because people were more credulous or scientifically unsophisticated in previous centuries. We have astrologers, Tarot readers, and *I Ching* software for the same reasons as the generations that invented them – we are insatiably curious about our own future and would like to control it if we could. The enduring mystery of time is currently being furiously addressed by scientists; investigations into further dimensions have recently inspired thousands of research papers and more than 200 international conferences. Evidence exists that, although we are familiar with three dimensions, there may be seven more, the existence of which seriously affects our current knowledge about the nature of time. The physicists' conclusions may or may not enlighten us, but it is doubtful that our fortune-tellers will need to put away their crystal balls – at least for the foreseeable future.

Ψ   Ψ

LEFT: The traditional materials assembled in preparation for an *I Ching* prediction.

CHAPTER VIII

WHAT HAPPENS NEXT?

ABOVE: **A 12th-century impression of the soul leaving the body at death.**

It is hard to accept that death means the eradication of a human being. In fact, few of us do believe that death is the end. People in most parts of the world choose to believe that death is merely the end of one phase of existence. Modern Western culture seems to be alone both in its lack of a coherent afterlife belief, and in allowing that death may be simply the end of it all; large numbers of contemporary Westerners seem to have no real convictions about what will happen to them after they die. But the absence of a definite set of beliefs does not mean that Westerners are without opinions on the subject. A casual glance at the media reveals both confusion and fascination. Traditional religious believers continue to assume the existence of afterlives of various sorts, but mainstream opinion seems to have lost this certainty. Despite there being no public assumption that there *is* an afterlife, we can read accounts of poltergeists in our newspapers, be invited to read novels written by authors after their deaths, and watch people under hypnosis on our television screens, describing in detail their previous lives. Hauntings seem to abound, especially in Europe. British real estate agents calmly discuss whether the existence of a ghost should be disclosed in the sale details of a property; failure to do so could anger a purchaser who later discovered the ghost, while describing a ghost who subsequently refused to appear could be equally problematic.

ABOVE: **An Aborigine vision of the dead, from rocks in the Northern Territory, Australia.**

THE CONCEPT OF SOUL OR SPIRIT

Faced with the various uncertainties that familiarity with other cultures has provoked, those Westerners who have little religious faith have tended to take an empirical view of the matter and expect to be convinced. Unfortunately, proof is hard to find.

Ψ  Ψ

LEFT: The dead rise from their graves in this Christian portrayal of the Resurrection.

ABOVE: **A medieval view of paradise**.

The question poses the same dilemma for everyone: there is no certain way of knowing what follows death. Despite this lack of evidence, societies in different times and places have evolved theories and beliefs which often bear striking resemblances. There is a common conviction that we are more than just our physical bodies, and that the individual life-force, the essence of our identity, is so strong that it survives the death of the body. It is the fate of this intangible part of the person, the soul or spirit, which is the concern of beliefs about the afterlife.

The separation of body and soul at death gives rise to problems in most belief systems; and the speed with which the separation takes place, as well as the destination of the soul, is not universally agreed upon. Nor is the role of the spirits of the dead in the lives of the living: sometimes they are thought to be malign, and sometimes helpful. West African societies traditionally accepted the involvement of the spirits in all aspects of everyday life and recognized a need to influence them where possible; other cultures, such as the Chinese, expect interference from the dead only when something has gone wrong. Most people agree that the dead have a specific place or places which sets them apart from the living.

ABOVE: A pre-Columbian paradise from Teotihucan.

Images of the land of the dead can be shaped by the earthly environment, as when some groups of Australian Aborigines imagined the spirits of their dead living on in caves bordering their territory. In Polynesia the dead have their own island, replete with the most beautiful animals and plants. Many cosmologies reflect a layered structure in which the underworld and the sky world offer alternative destinations for departed souls. The afterlife may be envisaged as a reflection of earthly life, often enhanced; the earliest-known burial sites include everyday objects for the use of the deceased, while the graves of the ancient rulers of Ur (now Iraq) contain the remains of an entire court.

The idea that merit in life determines the fate of the soul after death is not limited to the Christian tradition, where Heaven and Hell reflect the fate of the virtuous and the sinful – there is a more widespread feeling that our actions during earthly life carry over into death. The afterlife can take both pleasant and horrifying forms, as reward or punishment for earthly behavior. Both Islam and Hinduism connect actions on earth with the fate of the soul after death, and both the ancient Egyptians and the Zoroastrians envisioned a type of trial at which the sum of a life's behavior would be judged. For the Aztecs, it was the manner of dying that decided the soul's fate; those who died as a sacrifice to the gods went straight to paradise.

In most cultures it is felt that following death the body, after a suitable separation period, is redundant. It is clear to many that the body rapidly becomes unfit for further use, although it is often hard to imagine the form that the disembodied soul may subsequently take. The period directly after death is a problematic one, when a certain amount of ambiguity surrounds the deceased. They are still felt to have a place among the living, of whom they were so recently a part, and the balance between spirit, ancestor, and living member of the community is often not immediately resolved. An extreme expression of this feeling is seen among the traditional Dayak people of Borneo, who traditionally practice an elaborate death ritual in which the corpse has two funerals. At first the deceased is considered to be nearer to

167

ABOVE: **The embalmed body of Lenin, preserved for public display.**

the world of the living and the corpse is kept unburied, quite close to the village, to begin its process of decomposition. While this takes place, the spirit of the dead person is still too close to the living to enter the world of the ancestors. It is neither one thing nor the other, and is obliged to wander disconsolately in the vicinity of its corpse. Meanwhile relatives must make the spirit daily offerings and observe mourning rituals, as a discontented spirit will make trouble for everyone. By the time the corpse has reduced to bones the deceased is seen to have undergone his final change and is ready to enter the land of the ancestor spirits. This he does after a final funeral in which the bones are buried and the period of mourning ends.

Most other societies adopt less extreme ways of dealing with the transition, but in all cultures the funeral is important as marking the progress of the deceased from living to dead. Some feel that a longer marginal period is more helpful to the living, and we could interpret the increasingly popular modern Western custom of holding memorial services as something akin to the Dayak secondary funeral. Some months elapse after the initial funeral, in which grief and shock begin to pass and the deceased person gradually ceases to be thought of as alive; the memorial service then celebrates their life with a sense of acceptance and the deceased becomes "an ancestor."

When there is concern that the dead should not be thought of in the past tense huge efforts are made to preserve the corpse in life-like condition. The bodies of Lenin and Mao Zedong were not only embalmed but displayed. Death could not be denied, but the bodies remained as symbols of the leaders' metaphorical presence as long as this was required.

PRESERVING THE BODY IN THE AFTERLIFE

Not every culture has accepted the separation of body and soul, however. Native North Americans believe in a continuing association between the body and the spirit, and are currently campaigning for the return of the bones of their ancestors from archeological museums on these grounds. In the 3,000 years preceding the birth of Christ the Egyptians believed that the body was essential to proper progress into the afterlife. In Egyptian mythology the nature goddess Isis, wife of Osiris, god of the underworld, had to travel the land collecting the parts of his body that had been scattered by the god Seth. Only when she had done this and bandaged up the parts into a whole body could he be brought back to life. The ancient Egyptians' efforts to preserve the corpses of their dead have resulted in our most complete record of the artifacts, beliefs, and lifestyle of an ancient culture.

With the necessity to preserve the body came the need to protect and provision it for eternity. The extensive (and effective) measures which were taken meant that the main impression we have of ancient Egypt is of a people obsessed with death, funerals, and corpses. Our view is distorted by the fact that it is the funerary items which have survived; the Egyptians have become victims of their own success. Although we think of the tombs first, the statues, paintings, and artifacts preserved within them tell of a developed culture rich in art and music, and wealthy enough to support an aristocratic caste in considerable luxury. For a prosperous society, there seemed no better way to spend money than on making sure of eternal life. Death was not seen as the end; it was a stage in an ongoing process, but a stage fraught with risk and danger.

The Egyptians may have begun to think in this way because of the remarkable way in which the local desert sand preserved bodies buried in it. It may have appeared likely to those who accidentally discovered the life-like corpses in the sand that the bodies were still in use, and from this sprang the notion that the spirit needed a place to rest in its continuing life. They did not believe that the body could so rapidly become redundant. The relationship between the physical and spiritual was thought to be more complex, with the body central to continuance into the afterlife. Egyptian

ABOVE: Isis, standing behind her husband Osiris. In Egyptian mythology she gathered up his body and bandaged it so that he could be restored to life.

notions of the soul were complex; there were two aspects, the *ka*, or life force, and the *ba*, the more personal identity of the deceased. Both *ba* and *ka* left the body at death. The *ka* returned to the body and the tomb and needed continuing gifts of food and other offerings to sustain it, as well as the ritual services of a priest to give magical protection, while the *ba* journeyed to the underworld where it underwent various ordeals in order to become an *akh*, a semidivine spirit. Without a body to use as a base the spirit would be forced to stay in the cold, dark, comfortless wastes of the Land of the Dead.

The central theme of Egyptian belief was the unification of all aspects of the person after death; only then could they move successfully into the eternal light of the afterlife. There was much that could be done to ensure this progress – preserving the body, providing continuing offerings and ensuring magical protection – but only the wealthy and powerful could expect this level of attention. They started preparations in advance of their death, setting aside land, not just for their tomb, but to supply the offerings and pay for the rituals which would ensure their immortality. For the mightiest in the land no effort was spared. A dead Pharaoh enjoyed a rich and complex burial: the Pyramids, the world's most dramatic and imposing monuments, were constructed for their exclusive benefit. These staggering engineering achievements were intended not only as memorials but as the launching pad for the perfected *akh* or essence of the deceased Pharaoh to take its place among the gods.

THREATS FROM THE DEAD

Oblivion seemed the worst of all fates to an Egyptian; it was a duty to remember the dead and keep making offerings and spells, which helped them progress smoothly into the eternal afterlife. To fail in this transition and to be eradicated from human memory meant eternal cold and darkness, a fate regarded with horror and fear.

It has been suggested that the attention given by Egyptians to death and the after-life may be connected to the generally early age of death which examination of the mummies has revealed; most were less than 40 when they died, and all seemed to have suffered heavily from parasitic infections. Since life on earth tended to be short and often unhealthy, the appeal of an afterlife was perhaps understandable to those who could afford to avoid early oblivion. It was also true that the Egyptians feared the consequences of failing to pay proper attention to their dead; unless safely seen throught the transition, a spirit could cause illness and misfortune for its living rela-tives. A story from the second millennium BC tells how the High Priest of Amun-Ra in Thebes tracked down the source of some local trouble to an unquiet *akh* whose tomb had been neglected. The priest ordered immediate reparation and promised the *akh* further funerary offerings. Only then could life in Thebes returns to normal. The magic spells used freely throughout Egyptian life also took account of the threat from the dead. Various parts of the house had spells and formulae on their walls to guard against wandering ghosts whose progress to the Land of the Dead had been interrupted.

The earliest-known Egyptian graves contained personal items, and as time progressed provision for the afterlife became more elaborate. Sand burials were inappropriate for these kind of complicated funerals, but attempts to provide more dignity, space, and protec-tion for the corpse led to the opposite result – the corpses, out of contact with the sand, quickly decomposed. Experiments in search of different meth-ods of preserving the corpses were con-ducted; the result was the development of a remarkable system of embalming which has allowed corpses to remain in life-like condition for more than 3,000 years. Not all attempts succeeded: the word "mummy" derives from the Arabic word for bitumen or pitch, and was first

BELOW: The Egyptian mummification technique was a lengthy process performed by skilled specialists.

ABOVE: The weighing of the heart, as recorded in the papyrus Book of the Dead, about 1300 BC.

Ψ used when travellers saw early mummies which were blackened with resin; they assumed that bitumen had been used in the process. In fact natron was the main preserving agent used in a lengthy and skilled process which reached its peak in the 10th and 11th centuries BC.

Archeological evidence reveals that magic was important in Egyptian life; it was complex and powerful, embodying principles which have been the foundations of many subsequent systems, including alchemy and Rosicrucianism. It was equally prominent in death. Ritual surrounded all stages of the embalming process, which appears to have been seen as an essential caring service, equivalent to healing in the living. Magic was thought to be equally necessary in the afterlife, judging from the numerous spells left for the use of the dead person. There were spells to avoid "perishing in the Land of the Dead" as well as detailed spells for all possible afterlife emergencies – they seemed to constitute an essential handbook to cope with the difficulties of the journey. Texts and images on the coffins, tomb walls, and artifacts were all essential components; the preserved mummy was only one part of the equation. Incantations found on chamber entrances guarded against harmful animals. Maps of the land of Osiris were inscribed on the coffin walls to guide the spirit of the deceased. Later tombs have all these spells and instructions written out in what came to be known as the "Book of the Dead." As well as a body, food, clothing, and other items, the newly dead spirit needed the magical spells contained in these papyrus sheets. Only with the help of these texts could the dead person achieve the final ambition and become an *akh*, at one with the world of sun, light, and eternity.

One of the obstacles along the way was the Judgement of the Dead, when the actions of the deceased during life were, literally, weighed alongside his or her heart in the balance. It was the role of the deceased vigorously to deny any wrongdoing, and if he or she was truthful, the heart, placed in the scales, would not outweigh a feather. If it did, the heart would be devoured by the monster Ammit, and eternal life would come to a full stop. If the deceased passed the test, they could go on into the afterlife. It was thus essential that the heart should be preserved after death, and it

ABOVE: A Thai spirit house, in which offerings are made to the spirits of the dead.

LEFT: The gold mummy mask of the young Pharaoh Tutankhamun, discovered in his almost intact tomb in 1922.

was always placed back inside the mummy, often with magical scarab beetles for protection. These proved not to be effective against grave robbers, who regularly made holes in the chests of the mummies to extract the scarab, which although carved from stone, was often set in gold.

The Egyptians believed strongly in the power of images and, since they used hieroglyphics, in the written word. Often the mere presence of an image or incantation was thought to be magically effective. Amulets were put in the tomb to protect the deceased, and it was thought that pictures of certain animals and objects were enough to make them available in the afterlife. The various masks, portraits, and statues of the deceased could also be fallbacks in the afterlife if preservation of the body was imperfect.

Consciousness of the role of magic in the burials, as well as the belief in an avenging *akh,* lay behind the notion that entering the tombs could be dangerous. It was in the interests of the relatives of the dead to reinforce this belief since one of the main problems was grave robbers, who broke into the tombs and stole the vital artifacts and texts and desecrated the mummies in their search for precious amulets. Robbery destroyed all the careful preparations made for the deceased and threatened his passage to the afterlife, so the entrances to tombs were carefully hidden and sealed and magic employed to protect the tomb against intruders. Although this did not stop all the grave robbers, particularly in later centuries, it did give rise to a popular belief among Westerners that those who opened a Pharaoh's tomb would suffer the mummy's curse. Egyptian magic was respected but little understood – a potent threat for those about to break in upon the highest achievement of that art. There was a feeling that the mummies were not dead in the Western meaning of the word, but repositories of supernatural power.

These remained generalized fears until the discovery of the tomb of Tutankhamun in the Valley of the Kings in 1922. This was a staggering find, as the tomb was the untouched resting place of a Pharaoh; to enter it meant going back thousands of years in time. Various political difficulties surrounded the opening of the tomb, but a further problem presented itself as the idea of the curse unfolded. It was first proposed by the novelist Marie Corelli, who provoked shivers of excitement by writing to the *Times* newspaper in London to share her discovery of a curse in an ancient Arabic text. Days later Lord Carnavon, the sponsor of the discovering expedition, died from an infected mosquito bite sustained when coming out of the tomb. Instantly the curse became an established fact, with every possible misfortune being linked to it. It was even suggested that the curse was inscribed on the walls of the tomb, which was untrue.

From the moment of Carnavon's death the story gathered momentum; every unfortunate event such as a power failure in Cairo at the time of Lord Carnavon's death, and the simultaneous death of his dog at his English home, was meticulously chronicled and published. Collectors who possessed objects from other Egyptian tombs decided that it was unsafe to keep them, and the British Museum received a succession of anonymous parcels. Over the following 10 years more than 20 of those associated with the Tutankhamun tomb opening died of various causes, but the chief player in the affair, the archeologist Howard Carter, who had discovered the tomb and was the first person actually to enter it, remained in excellent health and died peacefully years later. Whatever magical secrets were known to the ancient Egyptians, it seems unlikely that they were ever directed toward the actors in this 20th-century drama.

The Egyptians were not unique in viewing their dead as potentially threatening, or in thinking it essential that the dead be happily settled in their afterlife. For the Chinese, illness and misfortune can often be attributed to the discontented spirits of the dead. Even in Western-influenced areas such as Hong Kong and Taiwan, ghost beliefs are deep-seated. The spirits of the dead are thought to dwell in the Land of the Shades, where their level of existence depends on factors such as the manner of their dying, their virtue in life, and the attention they receive from their descendants. The most comfortable spirits are those who become contented ancestors; they generally lived to old age, and have large families of descendants who make regular sacrifices, remember them in rituals, and maintain their memorial tablet on the family altar. The essential offerings consist of food and drink, and paper fascimiles of money and artifacts which are burned; their essence is received by the spirit as the smoke rises. Taiwanese shops specialize in complex and beautifully made paper houses, with miniature objects and furnishings, which are bought to be offered to ancestors and gods. Ancestors of special virtue may, after a period of accruing more merit in the afterlife, become gods. As such they may be remembered by and receive sacrifices from more than their immediate kin group, thus increasing their chances of eternal comfort and power.

Ψ

Ψ

Ψ

Ψ

UNEASY SPIRITS

Some classes of Chinese spirits are not so fortunate; instead of proceeding serenely toward becoming an ancestor they move uneasily in and out of the world of the living as ghosts. Some, such as those who died violently or in accidents, are caught in a situation beyond their control. It is thought that car crash victims are trapped near the scene of their death until another death takes place there – only then can the first victim progress to the Land of the Shades. Similarly, those who die from drowning can only leave when another spirit can be found to take their place. For this reason the scenes of accidents and violence are thought extremely dangerous to the living, who may be drawn to their own deaths. The most dangerous ghosts are those of suicides, who are in pursuit of revenge. A woman can strike terror in all who know her by committing suicide wearing her wedding dress, a clear declaration of her intention to cause harm after death.

Chinese spirits who have become ancestors, but whose family are neglecting their duties, may be forced to become ghosts to remedy their position. Without offerings from the living, the ancestors suffer extremes of poverty and discomfort and in desperation and anger intrude into the life of their descendants. A typical story from the anthrpologist David Jordan, who worked in Taiwan, describes a village girl who was visited in the fields by the ghost of her father, dressed in rags and complaining of his pitiable condition. The girl, alarmed and distressed, returns home to make immediate

175

offerings to the deprived ancestor. Given the essential nature of the sacrifices, it follows that the most unfortunate category of spirits are those who have died young, without having children, or whose descent line has died out and left them without descendants to sacrifice to them. Such spirits become "hungry ghosts," troublesome and restless, and sacrifices are often left at doorways to placate such ghosts and deflect their malevolence. There are ways for a ghost to remedy even such a dire situation, and the most common is a still-flourishing institution known as ghost marriage.

The first sign that something is wrong, and a ghost is demanding action, is generally persistent ill-health or a string of illnesses among family members. A visit to a diviner will be required to pinpoint the problem; one of the questions he will ask is whether the family has a child who has died without marriage or children. The diviner then decides if the ghost of this child is trying to attract attention because it wants its situation remedied. If the answer is yes, the family will decide to secure a descent line for the ghost. A male deceased person can adopt sons postmortally; these would normally be provided by a brother. The new sons retain their kin and legal ties to their biological father, but take on ritual obligations to their adoptive father: putting his memorial tablet upon their own altar, they agree to recognize him as their ancestor and make sacrifices to his spirit.

The situation with female unmarried ghosts is more complex, since Chinese descent is through the male line and a woman takes her descent line from her husband. If unmarried, she is marginal in the kin structure, as she does not properly belong to her parents' line, and even the presence of her memorial tablet on their altar causes embarrassment. It is thus impossible for an unmarried woman to have descendants or to adopt children. The only solution is to find a husband to marry the ghost. There are various ways of choosing one. As the marriage is ritual rather than legal, it does not affect the bridegroom's existing marriage. In some areas the groom is likely to be the husband of the dead girl's sister. Elsewhere the groom may be found by leaving an invitation in a red envelope on the road. As red is the colour of money gifts, sooner or later someone will pick it up and respond to the request. A dowry will normally be offered as inducement. The wedding itself is similar to a real one, involving the bride's family in considerable expense; the dead bride may be represented by her memorial tablet or by an effigy in bridal clothes. The new husband then takes the girl's memorial tablet to his own altar and, including her with his ancestors, makes offerings as if she were his dead wife. This resolution usually brings profound relief to the dead girl's family, and the misfortunes which prompted the action seem then to evaporate.

GHOSTLY APPARITIONS AND POLTERGEISTS

Both the Egyptian and Chinese spirits fit firmly into a cosmology of the afterlife, but even without such a clear-cut system the souls of the dead must reach their destination safely for all to be well. Funeral ritual can be crucial: incorrect burial can mean that the spirit is unable to proceed and will make its presence known among the living as a ghost. The Greek philosopher Athenodorus, who lived in the 1st century BC, took cheap lodgings which were reputed to be haunted. He found himself sharing his house with a ghost who wore chains and seemed to be in distress. Having noticed where the ghost disappeared, Athenodorus started to dig and discovered a chained skeleton. Surmising that the skeleton was the hastily concealed victim of a murder, Athenodorus had the remains properly buried; the ghost was not seen again. Athenodorus's ghost was the precursor of numerous spirits who in succeeding centuries seem to have directed human attention to their various improperly buried remains.

Ghosts can be spirits unable to proceed further because of some score they have to settle with the living. Those who have been murdered, especially if the murder was concealed or

Ψ

LEFT: The Greek philosopher Athenodorus sees the chained ghost in his house. His account became the first recorded ghost story.

ABOVE: The ghost of Hamlet's father appears on the battlements.

unavenged, have restless spirits who linger as ghosts until they receive acknowledgement. In Shakespeare's plays spirits return to torment the living and prevent their deaths being ignored. The ghost of Hamlet's father declared that he was doomed to wander until "the foul crimes done in my days of nature are burnt and purged away." The haunting may be as much a reproach and a warning as a demand for justice. Banquo's bloodied ghost appears at Macbeth's feast to remind him of the horror of his crimes, and Caesar's ghost appears to herald Brutus's inevitable violent end.

Striking guilt and horror in the living seems to be the object of this type of ghost's appearance. In 1779 the British aristocrat Lord Thomas Lyttleton had a night-time visit from the ghost of a previous mistress. After his heartless abandonment of her she had committed suicide, and was returning now to tell him of his own death, the day and hour of which she announced. As the time approached he became extremely agitated and his friends, unconvinced of the seriousness of his apparition, advanced the time of his clocks so that he could get some peace. He was delighted to find himself still alive after his clocks had struck the predicted hour, and soon headed happily for bed, unaware of the real time. But at the exact moment predicted by the ghost of his mistress he suddenly collapsed and died.

Ghosts are generally thought of as people, but some ghostly apparitions include the physical objects in which the deaths took place. Thus ghost ships, phantom coaches, and even unearthly trains have all been recorded. The airfield at Biggin Hill, England, from which hundreds of Royal Air Force missions were flown during World War II is occasionally visited by a phantom fighter. Local residents see and hear the Spitfire coming in to land, although no real plane actually does so. It is believed to represent a ghostly connection with the many young men who took off from the airfield and never returned.

Very occasionally long-gone buildings may reappear. In 1926, in Suffolk, England, two women were out walking in the villages surrounding their new home. They were interested by an imposing Georgian house set in large gardens and surrounded by a wall, and were subsequently surprised that no one locally seemed to know of it. Some time later they repeated their walk, only to discover that there was no trace of either

BELOW: In Shakespeare's play *Julius Caesar*, the ghost of Caesar appears to the guilty Brutus.

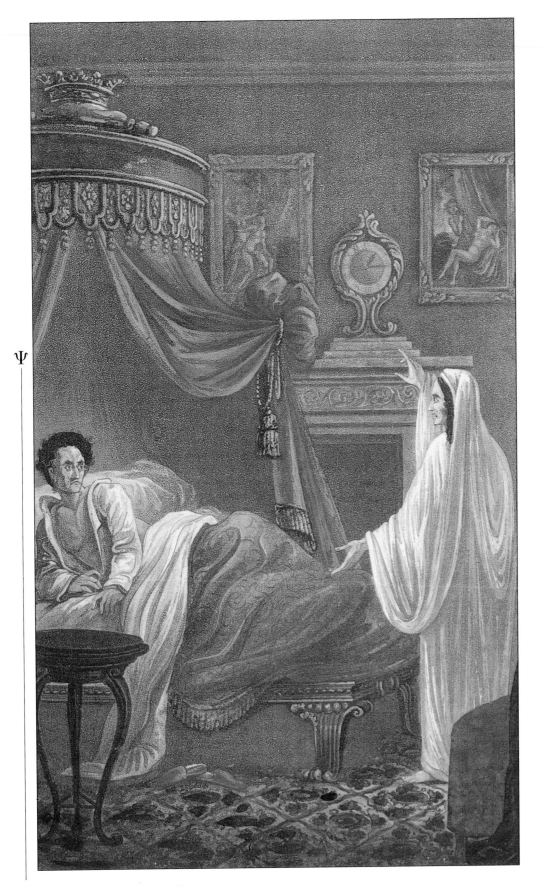

Ψ

Ψ

LEFT: A ghostly apparition tells Lord Lyttleton of his imminent death, a prophesy that turned out to be fulfilled.

ᴪ

ᴪ

ABOVE: **The ghost of Jane Seymour is often seen at this spot, near the private stairway which in her lifetime led to her apartments.**

house or grounds – only a site that had long been derelict. Both women were certain of what they had seen and were stunned by the house's disappearance. They were regarded as reliable witnesses and had no feeling that there was anything strange about the house on their original visit. Explanations have ranged from a joint hallucination, through hysterical attention-seeking, to an apparition out of time, but the mystery was never solved.

There are buildings which themselves seem to attract hauntings. Sometimes this is because violent or tragic events have taken place there; Hampton Court, in England, has seen the ghosts of Jane Seymour, who died just after giving birth to Henry VIII's son, and Catherine Howard, another of his six wives, whose vain attempts to beg for Henry's mercy before her execution are said to be re-enacted in the gallery of the house. Other ancient evils live on in old houses and castles, such as Glamis Castle in Scotland which is haunted by an early Lady Glamis as well as the aftermath of the "Glamis Horror," a story referring to a secret locked room in which an unspeakable act of violence is said to have taken place. One of the most famous buildings in recent times was a Dutch Colonial-style house in Amityville, New York, the scene of the frightening hauntings which formed the basis for the film, *The Amityville Horror*. But houses do not have to be old to have ghosts. Of the numerous regular reports of ghost and poltergeist activity, many come from modern houses, flats, and even offices and shops.

Exorcisms, in which ministers of the Church are asked to banish ghosts from buildings, are often effective in stopping haunting activity. A hotel in Perthshire, Scotland, was successfully exorcised in 1994 after ghostly sightings and constant, inexplicable damage during renovations.

Poltergeists have just as long a history as ghosts. Instead of manifesting as visual apparitions, poltergeists make noises and move objects, creating confusion among the living. The word itself, from the German, means "noisy spirit." An early poltergeist report came from the German village of Bingen-am-Rhein in AD355 when there was an outbreak of unexplained noises, knocks, and stone-flying. Sporadic reports continued across Europe in succeeding centuries; some of them included the most common feature of poltergeist episodes – the presence of young adolescents, usually girls. A 14th-century incident in France, for example, concerned a young nun who, in addition to being the centre of the usual noises, blows, and flying objects, was often lifted up into the air. Families visited by poltergeists in later centuries include that of John Wesley, British founder of the Methodist Church, whose childhood home at Epworth, Lincolnshire, was occupied by a noisy spirit presence during 1716 and 1717. The Wesleys were a large family, including at this time two teenage sisters, one of

whom, Hetty, seemed to be the centre for the poltergeist activity. There was no physical connection between the noises, which were extremely varied and convincing, and the girl, and no explanation was ever found for the events, which John later wrote up in a published account. The happenings ceased, after two months, as suddenly as they had begun.

ABOVE: John Wesley, whose childhood home was the scene of poltergeist activity.

The connection between poltergeist activity and the spirits of the dead is not always obvious, although some cases suggest it. The Fox family disturbances in Hydesville, USA, led to a dialogue with the spirit concerned and the discovery of its skeleton, while the Borley Rectory case had a similar outcome. Borley Rectory was an English house, built in about 1863, in which supernatural events were reported over a long period. Apparitions were seen including that of a nun, but most of the nuisance came from noises, blows, flying objects, and unexplained breakages. In 1929 Harry Price, a renowned British psychic investigator, went to the Rectory to carry out inquiries, none of which were conclusive. During the 1930s the house was occupied by the Reverend Lionel Foyster, his wife, and their young child. Poltergeist activity reached a new intensity, with Mrs Foyster apparently the main victim, although the events were seen, heard, and felt by many other witnesses. In the late 1930s, during the course of Price's continuing investigations of the phenomena, a seance was held which brought a message from a spirit, apparently describing her murder in the Manor House which had once occupied the site of the Rectory. A later seance brought the prediction that the Rectory would shortly burn down, and that the cause of the hauntings would be discovered under the cellar. Somewhat later than the prediction, Borley Rectory did indeed catch fire. When it was eventually demolished, investigators

RIGHT: The ruin of
Borley Rectory after it
had been swept by
fire.

RIGHT: The ruin of
Borley Rectory after it
had been swept by
fire.

Ψ   Ψ

excavated the foundations and uncovered the skeleton of a woman in her thirties.

Ghosts and poltergeists cut across all descriptive categories and seem to defy a general explanation. They are seen at all times of day in all sorts of places, their demeanor sometimes dramatic, sometimes nondescript, appearing mostly to individuals but occasionally to groups. The only positive thing that can be said is that they have been known from earliest times in all parts of the world, and that those who have seen, felt, or heard them are totally convinced of the validity of their experience. A survey conducted in Britain at the beginning of the century by the Society for Psychical Research revealed that over six per cent of the cross-section of the population who were interviewed had experienced some kind of ghost encounter. Any social gathering contains individuals who can produce accounts of these experiences, often first-hand. But objective proof is hard to establish; even where they have appeared to more than one person at the same time it cannot be proved that collusion, hypnosis, or hallucination were not involved. Ghost hunters have set out with all the paraphernalia of recording equipment and cameras but have, unsurprisingly, often failed in their task. Where recordings and photographs have been made, and the obvious frauds dismissed, there remain some manifestations that cannot be explained. But it is possible that they are simply better fakes or accidental illusions, and they cannot constitute scientific evidence. As with so many aspects of the supernatural, experience is the only convincing evidence, and personal experience is not transferable.

PAST LIVES

The end of mortal life may, of course, merely be a point at which the soul or spirit transfers from an extinguished body to a new one. Reincarnation is a key belief in major religions such as Hinduism and Buddhism, and appears in the beliefs of societies as far apart as the ancient Greeks, the Pacific Islanders, the central Australian Aborigines and the native peoples of North, Central, and South America. The idea takes different forms. Hindus believe that repeated incarnations are necessary for the soul to reach spiritual perfection; progress is rewarded by a rise in the status of each incarnation, thus legitimizing the position of high-caste Brahmins who are thought to be the most ritually pure members of mainstream Hindu society. Buddhism also stresses the goal of spiritual progress, culminating in the achievement of complete detachment from worldly desires and concerns. This is achieved in the course of many incarnations in which the individual life-force, rather than the personality, is the element which is continued. In both of these religions, reincarnation does not necessarily imply an immediate transfer from body to body, although this is sometimes thought to occur; the soul is allowed a time of either limbo or atonement. Neither is it generally thought by Buddhists that memories of past lives are available to individuals – except occasionally children, who are less firmly rooted in their present lives.

None of the mainstream Judeo-Christian religions includes reincarnation in its teaching, yet a 1981 Gallup poll in England revealed that 23 per cent of its sample believed that it was possible to be reborn. An earlier Gallup poll in the United States produced similar results. These interesting statistics indicate that many people are attracted to the idea, even without a religious setting. Some Western believers describe the notion of a recycling of spirit or mind energy: our soul material is contained on the earth in finite amounts, like water or carbon, and, like energy, can change its form while being neither created nor destroyed. Belief may be linked to regular media reports of those who appear to have memories of other lives. These accounts attract considerable attention and seem very compelling; they are convincing enough to make many people reluctant to rule out the possibility of reincarnation.

Of those who seem able to recall past lives, the majority do so only under hypnosis. Sometimes the subjects speak with a different accent, or even in a different language, and talk of places, events, and details of which, in their conscious lives, they have no knowledge. Both subject and hypnotherapist frequently find this an astonishing, almost frightening experience, but more sober reflection can reveal other factors at work. The hypnotic state is one of extreme suggestibility, and subjects have been found to go to great lengths to produce responses which they believe are required. Hypnosis seems to give access to extensive, deeply stored memory, while releasing powerful imaginative capacities. This is an unfortunate mixture for those who wish to establish the accuracy of the recollections.

One of the most interesting cases in recent years was that of a Colorado housewife who in the early 1950s, under hypnosis, spoke as Bridey Murphy, an Irish woman of the 19th century. In a pronounced Irish accent, she described the events of her life, including details of everyday living. The hypnotherapist involved, Morey Bernstein, wrote a book called *The Search for Bridey Murphy,* and after its publication researchers began to check the accuracy of her descriptions. Some were found to be verifiable, although some crucial ones, such as her birth and death and the location and type of her house, were not.

Some details, such as the existence of a St Theresa's church, were correct, but did not tally with the date of her story. It then came to light that, although brought up by non-Irish relatives, the woman had spent the first three years of her life with her part-Irish parents. It seems likely that the Irish accent and the store of local Irish detail had come from childhood stories, recalled and embroidered in response to the hynotherapist's admitted questions. The ability to recall from such a young age is borne out by cases where adults who have spoken a language in infancy, and then been removed from it, are able to speak it under hypnosis. Yet when conscious they can neither speak nor understand the first language.

The existing accounts of past lives all reiterate the dilemmas of Bridey's case. The role of hypnosis itself comes under suspicion; most of us have huge reservoirs of stored information which we cannot consciously recall and would not necessarily recognize. A British regression therapist working in the 1970s had a subject who recalled two earlier lives. One of them was a Roman woman of around AD286. The recall of these lives was dramatic and impressive, but subsequent research discovered the details of the Roman life to be virtually identical to those in a somewhat obscure novel published in 1947. The subject had no recollection of ever seeing or reading the book, but the similarity is so complete that it is assumed that it had formed part of the woman's unconscious "information bank." It seems that details recalled and used in this way are perceived as vivid and real by the subjects, who do not recognize them as absorbed from another source. Such cases seriously undermine the arguments for taking memories recalled under hypnosis at face value, no matter how deeply felt they may appear to be.

Although occurring less often, memories of past lives recalled without hypnosis are just as powerful for the subject. Usually they come from children, who suddenly express strong feelings toward certain objects and places and claim, quite matter-of-factly, to remember things from another existence. These convictions tend to fade with age, but there is a case of an English woman, born in 1903, who from early childhood identified strongly with a particular period of Egyptian history in which she was convinced she had lived. The child, Dorothy Eady, even pinpointed her "home" – a temple built by Seti I. She appeared to have considerable knowledge of Egyptian life and a facility for reading and writing hieroglyphics. Her conviction increased as she grew up, and she married an Egyptian and settled in Egypt. Toward the end of her life she finally reached her "home" – the site of Seti's temple at Abydos – and with a deep feeling of fulfillment and contentment resolved to become one of its devotees and never to leave it again.

Ψ OPPOSITE: A 19th-century Tibetan mandala, illustrating the period between death and reincarnation.

THE ULTIMATE PROBLEM

Throughout the cases of previous life memories there is little that constitutes convincing evidence that a personality has been reborn. Yet many of us allow the benefit of the doubt to come down on the side of the possibility that reincarnation can occur. Belief in reincarnation is less a response to evidence than a deeply felt human sense that there is a continuation of individual life in some form. It is this conviction which has led to such interest in recent years in the similarity of "near death" sensations experienced by people who had suffered medical emergencies, including heart stoppages, before being revived by medical technology. Recurring images of swirling tunnels, an approaching light, and even a welcoming white figure tempted many

Ψ

Ψ

into hoping that these individuals were the perfect witnesses – the only voyagers into the afterlife to have returned with a description. Unfortunately there have been no further advances, and there is some evidence to suggest that the impressions are the physiological reaction of a dying brain, replicable by chemical and electrical means. And it must be remembered that the patients were not dead, only near to death; if brain activity had completely ceased they would not have been revivable. Individuals who have undergone the experience have in general found it deeply moving and significant – but yet again, the revelation cannot be shared.

We may be no nearer to discovering what awaits us after death, but it still seems important not to rule out the possibility that *something* does. Perhaps, even in the cynical modern world, not so many of us are ready to accept death as the final putting out of the light.

Death presents us with the last problem in our relationship with the unknown. We are no closer to understanding it than our earliest ancestors were; all we have gained is a firmer idea of what we do not know, and this is just as true for other areas of the supernatural. As with so much of what we cannot explain, we are thrown back on our personal experiences, through which we try vainly to convince others. An examination of these experiences throughout the vast range of societies on our planet shows that the questions, and some of the answers, are universal – as much a part of human existence as eating and tool-making. It may be that the operation of the supernatural is unknowable; we pursue it because what we think, believe, and do about it has importance in our lives. If this is so, we must consider the fate of modern Western society, as it is generally conceived, to be an unenviable one; with the decline of the major religions and a public undervaluing of spiritual and mystical matters there would seem to be little opportunity to fulfill these needs.

In fact, however, it emerges that mystical thinking is still very much alive in the West during the late 20th century; and that interest, however diverse, unformalized, and fragmentary, is taken in virtually any area into which the action of the supernatural may enter. Even the staunchest defenders of rationalism often unconsciously treat science itself as a faith, unquestioningly accepting its tenets without meaningful proof. Other groups and individuals pursue successions of fashions in supernatural belief, and employ the timeless elements of magic in socially acceptable ways. In all the avenues explored here, there is no evidence that any society ignores, or has ever ignored, the supernatural, or has been prepared to strip itself of those beliefs which it cannot verify. The nature of the beliefs may change, but the fact of their existence remains – it is an essential part of the quality of human experience.

INDEX

PICTURE ACKNOWLEDGEMENTS

The Authors and Publisher wish to thank the following for the pictures which appear in this book:

p.2:Birmingham City Museums and Art Gallery, courtesy of The Bridgeman Art Library; p.7:Kyoryokukai, Tokyo National Museum; p.10: left, Sarah Errington, courtesy of The Hutchinson Library, right Cafe Productions Ltd; p.11: Cafe Productions; p.12: Cafe Productions; p.13: John Hatt, courtesy of The Hutchinson Library; p.14: Mary Evans Picture Library; p.15: Cafe Productions; p.16: Mary Evans Picture Library; p.17: left, Mary Evans Picture Library, right, Associated Press; p.18: above, Cafe Productions, below, Cafe Productions; p.19: The Hutchinson Library; p.20: Images Colour Library; p.21: John Massey Stewart; p.22: Hamburg Ethrigraphic Museum, courtesy of John Massey Stewart; p.24: Fortean Picture Library; p.25: Mary Evans Picture Library; p.26: above, Images Colour Library, below, Fortean Picture Library; p.27: above, Mary Evans Picture Library, below, Mary Evans Picture Library; p.28: above,Mary Evans Picture Library, below,Mary Evans Picture Library; p.29: above, Fortean Picture Library, below, Society for Psychical Research, courtesy of Mary Evans Picture Library; p.30: Society for Psychical Research, courtesy of Mary Evans Picture Library; p.31: Images Colour Library; p.32: left, Guy Lyon Playfair, courtesy of Fortean Picture Library, right, Guy Lyon Playfair, courtesy of Fortean Picture Library; p.33: Dr Elmer R Grober, courtesy of Fortean Picture Library; p.34: Guy Lyon Playfair,courtesy of Fortean Picture Library; p.35:Paul Fusco, courtesy of Magnum Photos Ltd; p.36: left, Lambeth Palace Library, London, courtesy of The Bridgeman Art Library, right CM Dixon; p.37: Museo Diocesano, Cortona, courtesy of The Bridgeman Art Library; p.38: Gillian Lawson, courtesy of The Bridgeman Art Library; p.39: Museo Di San Marco Dell'Angelico, Florence, courtesy of The Bridgeman Art Library; p.40: above, Kungl Biblioteque, below Kevin M'Clure, courtesy of Mary Evans Picture Library; p.41: Cambridge University Library, The Bridgeman Art Library; p.42: Prado, Madrid, courtesy of The Bridgeman Art Library; p.44: Ara Guler, courtesy of Magnum Photos Ltd; p.45: Dolf Huitsuker, courtesy of Thames and Hudson Ltd; Dolf Huitsuker, courtesy of Thames and Hudson Ltd; p.47: Associated Press; p.48: Ancient Art and Architecture Collection, p.49: Fortean Picture Library; p.50: left, Mary Evans Picture Library, right, Images Colour Library; p.51: Mary Evans Picture Library; p.52: Mary Evans Picture Library; p.53: above, B Regent, courtesy of The Hutchinson Library, below, Mary Evans Picture Library; p.54: left, Images Colour Library, right, Images Picture Library; p.55: Mary Evans Picture Library; p.57: The Guildhall Art Gallery, courtesy of The Bridgeman Art Library; p.58: Hulton Deutsch Collection Ltd; p.59: John P Kelly, courtesy of The Image Bank; p.60: Images Colour Library; p.61: Hulton Deutsch Collection Ltd; p.62: Images Colour Library; p.63: Mary Evans Picture Library; p.64: Fortean Picture Library; p.65: above, Images Picture Library, below, Images Picture Library; p.66: Images Picture Library, p.67: Ancient Art and Architecture Collection; p.69: Images Colour Library; p.70: Fortean Picture Library; p.71: Mary Evans Picture Library; p.72: Images Colour Library; p.73: Images Colour Library; p.74: left, K Rodgers, courtesy of The Hutchinson Library; right, CM Dixon; p.75: Mark Edwards, courtesy of Still Pictures; p.77: The Hutchinson Library; p.78: The Mansell Collection; p.79: The Mansell Collection; p.80: E.T. Archive; p.81: above, Images Colour Library, below Ancient Art and Architecture Collection; p.82:Biblioteque Nationale, Paris, courtesy of The Bridgeman Art Library; p.83: Mary Evans Picture Library; p.84: Mary Evans Picture Library; p.85: Michael K Nichols, Magnum Photos Ltd; p.87: Mohamed Arnin,courtesy of Robert Harding Picture Library; p.89: Mary Evans Picture Library; p.90: left,Hulton Deutsch Collection Ltd, right, Andre Singer; p.91: Mary Evans Picture Library; p.93: Fortean Picture Library; p.95: Mary Evans Picture Library; p.96: The Guildhall Art Gallery, The Bridgeman Art Library; p.97: Mary Evans Picture Library; p.98: Mary Evans Picture Library; p.100: Mary Evans Picture Library; p.101: right, Mary Evans Picture Library, left, Hulton Deutsch Picture Collection; p.102: right, The Mansell Collection; p.103: Images Colour Library; p.104: Fortean Picture Library; p.105: right, Mary Evans Picture Library, left, Mary Evans Picture Library; p.106: Images Colour Library; p.107: Images Colour Library; p.108: Mary Evans Picture Library; p.109: Images Colour Library; p.111: Museum Del Bildenden,Kunst, Leipzig, courtesy of The Bridgeman Art Library; p.112 Lambeth Palace Library, London, courtesy of The Bridgeman Art Library; p.114: Images Colour Library; p.115: The Stapleton Collection, courtesy of The Bridgeman Art Collection; p.116: Images Colour Library; p.117: Raymond Buckland, courtesy of Fortean Picture Library; p.118: left, Hulton Deutsch Picture Collection, right, Images Colour Library; p.119: Mary Evans Picture Library; p.120: Gavin Graham Gallery, London, courtesy of The Bridgeman Art Library; p.121: Ernst Haas, courtesy of Magnum Photos Ltd; p.122: Fortean Picture Library; p.123: Mary Evans Picture Library; p.124: Fortean Picture Library; p.125: Images Colour Library; p.126: The London Magazine, courtesy of Images Colour Library; p.127: Images Colour Library; p.128: Rene Dahinden, courtesy of Fortean Picture Library; p.129: left, Rene Dahinden, courtesy of Fortean Picture Library, right, Mary Evans Picture Library; p.130: Images Colour Library; p.131: left,Mary Evans Picture Library, right, Mary Evans Picture Library; p.132: The Maas Gallery, courtesy of The Bridgeman Art Library; p.133: left: Images Colour Library, right, Mary Evans Picture Library; p.134: left,Board of Trustees, courtesy of The Bridgeman Art Library, right, Loren Coleman, Fortean Picture Library; p.135: left, Mary Evans Picture Library, right, Mary Evans Picture Library; p.136: The Koebal Collection; p.137: Mary Evans Picture Library; p.138: Images Colour Library; p.139:left, Mary Evans Picture Library, right, The Koebal Collection; p.140: left, Mary Evans Picture Library, right, Hulton Deutsch Picture Collection; p.141: Images Colour Library; p.142: Hulton Deutsch Picture Collection; p.152: Mary Evans Picture Library; p.153: Images Colour Library; p.154: left, Images Colour Library, right, Mary Evans Picture Library; p.156: above, Mary Evans Picture Library, below, Mary Evans Picture Library; p.157: Fortean Picture Library; p.158: Mary Evans Picture Library; p.161: left, Images Colour Library, right, The Bridgeman Art Library; p.162: left,Mary Evans Picture Library, right, Images Colour Library; p.163: Images Colour Library; p.164: left, Jean Loup Charmet, right, Images Colour Library; p.165: The Bridgeman Art Library; p.166: The Bridgeman Art Library; p.167: Images Colour Library; p.168: David King Collection; p.169: Mary Evans Picture Library; p.170: Mary Evans Picture Library; p.171: The Bridgeman Art Library; p.172: left,Images Colour Library, right, The Hutchinson Library; p.174: Images Colour Library, p.175: The Hutchinson Library; p.177: left,Mary Evans Picture Library, right, The Mansell Collection; p.178: The Mansell Collection; p.179: Mary Evans Picture Library; p.180: Mary Evans Picture Library; p.181: Hulton Deutsch Picture Collection; p.182: Mary Evans Picture Library; p.185: The Victorian and Albert Museum, courtesy of The Bridgeman Art Library.